A GUIDE TO

THE WINTER'S TALE

The Shakespeare Handbooks

Guides available now:

- Antony and Cleopatra
- As You Like It
- The Comedy of Errors
- Cymbeline
- Hamlet
- Henry IV, Part 1
- Julius Caesar
- King Lear
- Macbeth
- Measure for Measure
- The Merchant of Venice
- The Merry Wives of Windsor
- A Midsummer Night's Dream
- Much Ado About Nothing
- Othello
- Richard II
- Romeo and Juliet
- The Tempest
- Twelfth Night
- The Winter's Tale

Further titles in preparation.

The Shakespeare Handbooks

A Guide to
The Winter's Tale

by Alistair McCallum

Upstart Crow Publications

First published in 2019 by
Upstart Crow Publications

Copyright © Alistair McCallum 2019

A CIP catalogue record for this book
is available from the British Library

ISBN 978 1 899747 15 3

www.shakespeare-handbooks.com

Setting the scene

Shakespeare wrote *The Winter's Tale* in or around 1610, when he was in his mid-forties. He was a member and shareholder of the King's Men, the country's most prestigious theatre company.

As well as the large open-air Globe Theatre, which had been the company's home since the start of the century, the King's Men had recently started performing in the Blackfriars Theatre, a smaller indoor space with an intimate, candlelit atmosphere. This venue offered exciting new possibilities in terms of sound, lighting, and special effects, all of which Shakespeare was quick to exploit in his later plays such as *The Winter's Tale*.

Recent years had seen the great tragedies of *Othello*, *King Lear* and *Macbeth*; however, at this stage in his life, Shakespeare seems to have taken a decisive step away from tragedy. The major plays written in these later years of his career – *Pericles*, *Cymbeline*, *The Winter's Tale*, and *The Tempest* – are variously referred to as the Late Comedies, the Tragicomedies, or the Romances. In these plays, elements of tragedy, comedy, pastoral, myth, and symbolism are mingled. There is a strong emphasis on father-child relationships; and the painful separation of family members is a recurring theme, ending with eventual homecoming, reconciliation, and redemption.

The plot of *The Winter's Tale* was based on a lurid, sensational story, *Pandosto*, by Robert Greene. (It was Greene who, twenty years before, had scathingly referred to Shakespeare – the young provincial newcomer who lacked a university education – as an 'upstart crow'.) Shakespeare transformed Greene's melodramatic tale into a rich, thought-provoking, magical piece of theatre:

"Shakespeare made his play out of a paperback romance about royalty, sex, scandal, sudden violent feelings, death, lost children ... In Shakespeare's hands the story becomes a profound play with an extraordinary range of ideas and feelings and tones, a complete living world, rich with challenging, beautiful and varied verse and fine prose. The play has the attractive air of having been written by a great artist who knows exactly what he is doing; who can handle everything, from tiny effects to big emotions, with ease and skill."

Levi Fox, *The Shakespeare Handbook*, 1987

Lifelong friends

The magnificent court of Sicilia is playing host to an important guest: Polixenes, king of Bohemia, is visiting Leontes, the Sicilian king.

The two men have been close friends since childhood. Now, however, their royal duties, and the distance between their kingdoms, mean that their meetings are rare and precious.

Winter has arrived, and the royal visit is nearing its end. Polixenes has been in Sicilia for several months now, and is due to return to Bohemia shortly.

Curtain up

Two kingdoms

In the court of king Leontes, in Sicilia, two noblemen are in conversation. One, Archidamus, is a companion of the visiting Bohemian king, while the other, Camillo, is a Sicilian courtier. They are discussing the possibility that, following the two kings' amicable reunion in Sicilia, Leontes is planning, in return, to visit his friend in Bohemia later in the year.

Archidamus is concerned that Bohemia will seem mean and insignificant in comparison with the splendour of Sicilia. Camillo dismisses his concerns, but Archidamus insists that he is simply being honest. He cannot find words to describe the welcome they have received from Leontes:

> *Archidamus:* ... you shall see, as I have said, great difference
> betwixt our Bohemia and your Sicilia ... Wherein our
> entertainment shall shame us, we will be justified in
> our loves;[1] for indeed –
> *Camillo:* Beseech you –
> *Archidamus:* Verily, I speak it in the freedom of my knowledge.
> We cannot with such magnificence – in so rare – I
> know not what to say.
>
> [1] *although we will not be able to entertain you*
> *adequately, we will make up for it with our love*

Their hospitality has been offered freely, insists Camillo, and Archidamus need not feel indebted in any way. The important thing is the strength of the bond between the two nations and their kings. Although visits have been relatively rare in the past, the relationship has been maintained through frequent gifts and letters between the two leaders.

Archidamus mentions Leontes' son, the young prince Mamillius, who is widely admired. Camillo agrees that the boy is a great asset to his country:

> Camillo: ... It is a gallant child; one that, indeed, physics the subject,[1] makes old hearts fresh. They that went on crutches ere [2] he was born desire yet their life to see him a man.[3]
>
> [1] *reinvigorates the people of Sicilia*
> [2] *before*
> [3] *hope to stay alive until he has grown to manhood*

Perhaps Camillo is exaggerating, suggests Archidamus; although the prince undoubtedly represents great promise for the future, the elderly will cling onto their lives with or without a good reason.

A change of heart   I, ii

In Leontes' palace, Polixenes is explaining to his friend that the time has come for him to return, reluctantly, to Bohemia. He has been in Sicilia for nine months, and it would take the same time again to thank him for his kindness. Instead, he can only offer one final word of thanks:

> Polixenes: Time as long again
> Would be filled up, my brother, with our thanks,
> And yet we should for perpetuity
> Go hence in debt.[1] And therefore, like a cipher,
> Yet standing in rich place,[2] I multiply
> With one 'we thank you' many thousands moe
> That go before it.
> Leontes: Stay[3] your thanks a while,
> And pay them when you part.
> Polixenes: Sir, that's tomorrow.
>
> [1] *I would still be forever in your debt*
> [2] *like a zero at the end of a large number*
> [3] *hold, save*

Polixenes is anxious about what may be happening in Bohemia in his absence; besides, he says, he does not wish to outstay his welcome. Leontes tries to persuade his friend to stay a little longer, but Polixenes insists that he must take his leave.

Leontes turns to his wife Hermione, who is heavily pregnant, and asks her if she can change their visitor's mind. She points out that news arrived only yesterday from Bohemia confirming that all was well. She appreciates that Polixenes is undoubtedly missing his son, but demands teasingly that he stay for another week. When her husband goes to Bohemia on his forthcoming visit, she promises that she will allow him to stay beyond his planned date even though it will be a painful sacrifice for her.

Hermione refuses to take no for an answer, and her playful cajoling finally succeeds. Polixenes agrees to stay for another week:

Polixenes: I may not, verily.[1]
Hermione: Verily?
                 You put me off with limber[2] vows. But I,
                 Though you would seek t'unsphere the stars with oaths,[3]
                 Should yet say 'Sir, no going'. Verily
                 You shall not go. A lady's 'verily' is
                 As potent as a lord's. Will you go yet?[4]
                 Force me to keep you as a prisoner,
                 Not like a guest: so you shall pay your fees[5]
                 When you depart, and save your thanks. How say you?
                 My prisoner? Or my guest? By your dread 'verily'
                 One of them you shall be.
Polixenes: Your guest then, madam.

[1] *truly, honestly*
[2] *limp, feeble*
[3] *even if you swore so violently that the stars left their orbits*
[4] *are you still determined to go?*
[5] *pay your jailer for your board and lodging*

Reminiscences

Delighted that their guest has agreed to stay longer, Hermione questions him good-humouredly about his childhood with her husband Leontes. Polixenes has fond memories of long, carefree days together:

> *Hermione:*   Come, I'll question you
>   Of my lord's tricks[1] and yours when you were boys.
>   You were pretty lordings[2] then?
> *Polixenes:*   We were, fair queen,
>   Two lads that thought there was no more behind
>   But such a day tomorrow as today,[3]
>   And to be boy eternal.

> [1] *games, pranks*
> [2] *handsome little fellows*
> [3] *our only idea of the future was another day like today;*
>   *nothing would ever change*

Hermione is curious to know whether her husband had been the more mischievous of the two. Polixenes insists that they were both harmless, innocent boys:

> *Hermione:*   Was not my lord
>   The verier wag[1] o'th' two?
> *Polixenes:* We were as twinned lambs that did frisk i'th' sun
>   And bleat the one at th'other: what we changed
>   Was innocence for innocence;[2] we knew not
>   The doctrine of ill-doing,[3] nor dreamed
>   That any[4] did.

> [1] *more of a rascal*
> [2] *all the words and thoughts we exchanged were*
>   *innocent*
> [3] *we had not learned to behave badly*
> [4] *anyone*

> *We were as twinned lambs that did frisk i'th' sun ...*
>
> *"Renaissance commentators were more inclined to discuss male–male friendship in the intimate and affectionate terms we might now reserve for romantic partnerships ... Many of Shakespeare's comedies dramatize marriage as the painful severing of strong male affections."*
>
> Laurie Maguire and Emma Smith, *30 Great Myths about Shakespeare*, 2013

At some point, suggests Hermione, they must have lost their innocence. Polixenes replies that temptation did not come until later, when he and Leontes met their future wives. In that case, Hermione retorts light-heartedly, giving in to temptation was forgivable as long as no one else was involved.

Leontes now comes over to join them. He is pleased, he tells his wife, that she has succeeded in persuading their friend to stay longer. He can only think of one occasion when her words were more effective:

> *Leontes:* Is he won yet?
> *Hermione:* He'll stay, my lord.
> *Leontes:* At my request he would not.
> Hermione, my dearest, thou never spok'st
> To better purpose.
> *Hermione:* Never?
> *Leontes:* Never, but once.

Hermione pretends not to understand, and demands that Leontes spell out exactly when this other occasion was. She craves praise and encouragement, she tells him jokingly, and will be delighted to know of the other time when her words were so meaningful.

She is pleased to hear that it was when she agreed, after an agonising wait, to marry him:

> *Leontes:*   Why, that was when
> Three crabbed[1] months had soured themselves to death
> Ere I could make thee open thy white hand
> And clap thyself my love.[2] Then didst thou utter,
> 'I am yours for ever.'
> *Hermione:* ... Why, lo you now,[3] I have spoke to th' purpose[4] twice.
> The one for ever earned a royal husband;
> Th'other for some while a friend.
>
> [1] *difficult, unpleasant*
> [2] *clasp my hand and pledge your love*
> [3] *that's remarkable*
> [4] *said the right thing*

With that, Hermione takes Polixenes' hand, and they resume their conversation.

An unspoken fear

It now becomes clear that Leontes, under his calm exterior, is burning with jealousy and suspicion. He observes Polixenes and Hermione closely, convinced that there is an intense sexual attraction between them:

> *Leontes:*   This entertainment
> May a free face put on[1] ...
> But to be paddling palms and pinching fingers,[2]
> As now they are, and making practised smiles
> As in a looking-glass; and then to sigh, as 'twere
> The mort o'th' deer[3] ...
>
> [1] *this hospitable treatment may wear an innocent expression*
> [2] *stroking palms and squeezing fingers*
> [3] *like the dying breath of a hunted deer*

Leontes calls for his son Mamillius. He tries to talk to the boy, but is drawn obsessively to the subject of Hermione. He even starts to doubt whether he is the boy's father, despite their clear resemblance:

Leontes: ... they say we are
        Almost as like as eggs[1] – women say so,
        That will say anything.

        [1] identical to one another

Scarcely able to contain his anguish, Leontes soon becomes visibly upset. His wife and Polixenes both notice his distress, and come to find out what is troubling him.

Leontes apologises, and explains that he sometimes becomes overly emotional when he looks at his son. He admits that his sentimentality can seem amusing to others:

Hermione: You look
        As if you held a brow of much distraction.
        Are you moved,[1] my lord?
Leontes: No, in good earnest.
        How sometimes nature will betray its folly,
        Its tenderness, and make itself a pastime
        To harder bosoms.[2] Looking on the lines
        Of my boy's face, methoughts I did recoil[3]
        Twenty-three years, and saw myself unbreeched,[4]
        In my green velvet coat ...

        [1] upset, angry
        [2] sometimes our natural feelings for our children
           result in excessive fondness, making us figures of
           fun to harder-hearted people
        [3] I felt as if I was taken back
        [4] too young to wear a man's breeches

Leontes asks his friend if he too is devoted to his young son. Polixenes replies that, when he is at home in Bohemia, he is forever in his boy's company. The child invigorates him, and prevents him from becoming melancholy:

Polixenes: If at home, sir,
He's all my exercise, my mirth, my matter; [1]
Now my sworn friend, and then mine enemy;
My parasite,[2] my soldier, statesman, all.
He makes a July's day short as December,
And with his varying childness cures in me
Thoughts that would thick my blood.[3]

[1] *my concern, the subject of all my thoughts*
[2] *flatterer, follower*
[3] *with his changing moods, he dispels any feelings of gloom or despair*

Leontes now asks Polixenes and Hermione to leave him alone with Mamillius. He instructs his wife to look after their guest well. As they leave for a walk in the garden, however, there is a hidden menace in his words:

Hermione: If you would seek us,
We are yours i'th' garden. Shall's attend you[1] there?
Leontes: To your own bents dispose you.[2] You'll be found,
Be you beneath the sky.[3]

[1] *shall we wait for you*
[2] *do whatever you want*
[3] *as long as the sky is above you; wherever you are*

Hermione offers Polixenes her arm, and the two of them leave, chatting amicably. Leontes watches, filled with loathing and disgust.

"Suspicions amongst thoughts are like bats amongst birds, they ever fly by twilight. Certainly they are to be repressed, or at least well guarded: for they cloud the mind; they lose friends; and they check with business ... They dispose kings to tyranny, husbands to jealousy, wise men to irresolution and melancholy ... in fearful natures they gain ground too fast. There is nothing makes a man suspect much, more than to know little ..."

Francis Bacon, *Of Suspicion*, 1625

Accusations

Alone with his young son, Leontes becomes even more tormented. He is by now certain that his wife is unfaithful to him. He orders Mamillius to go away and play on his own, reflecting bitterly that in time the boy, like everyone else, will regard him with scorn and ridicule:

> *Leontes:* Go play, boy, play. Thy mother plays,[1] and I
> Play too; but so disgraced a part, whose issue
> Will hiss me to my grave.[2] Contempt and clamour
> Will be my knell.[3]

> [1] *is playing sexual games; is adulterous*
> [2] *I am playing a role, but such a loathsome one that onlookers, including my own child, will jeer me off the stage*
> [3] *my funeral bell*

The world is full of men whose wives are unfaithful, he declares scathingly, though most do not know it. Adultery is everywhere, and there is no escape:

> *Leontes:*   Physic[1] for't there's none:
> It is a bawdy planet,[2] that will strike
> Where 'tis predominant;[3] and 'tis powerful, think it[4] ...

> [1] *medicine, a cure*
> [2] *the cause is the influence of the planet Venus, which provokes lust*
> [3] *take effect when the planet is in the ascendant*
> [4] *believe it*

Leontes calls for his adviser Camillo, and questions him about Polixenes. When Camillo agrees that everyone is aware that the king's guest is staying for a further week, Leontes seizes on his words. He is convinced that the entire court, and probably the populace in general, is aware of the queen's debauched behaviour.

He accuses Camillo of deliberately keeping him in the dark:

Camillo: I think most understand
     Bohemia[1] stays here longer.
Leontes: Ha?
Camillo: Stays here longer.
Leontes: Ay, but why?
Camillo: To satisfy your highness, and the entreaties[2]
     Of our most gracious mistress.
Leontes: Satisfy?
     Th'entreaties of your mistress? Satisfy?
     Let that suffice. I have trusted thee, Camillo,
     With all the nearest things to my heart …
           But we have been
     Deceived in thy integrity, deceived
     In that which seems so.[3]

[1] *the king of Bohemia, Polixenes*
[2] *appeals, requests*
[3] *deceived by your superficial air of honesty*

Hermione is no better than a common prostitute, states Leontes; and it is clear that Camillo, whether from cowardice, malice, or negligence, has been hiding the truth from him.

"Leontes seeks to disengage himself from the very ongoing nature of life. His is a cold spirit of negativism. Brooding like the winter on a procreative past, Leontes expresses his fear of time through hatred of sex, a hysterical misogyny, and obsessive threats of death."

Charles Frey, *Shakespeare's Vast Romance*, 1980

Camillo is horrified by the accusation, and equally shocked by Leontes' baseless slandering of the queen. If anyone other than the king had made such allegations, declares Camillo, he would immediately take revenge.

Leontes persists: he has noticed countless signs of infidelity, and it would be senseless to ignore them. His anger intensifies, and Camillo implores him to see reason:

> Leontes: Is whispering nothing?
> Is leaning cheek to cheek? Is meeting noses?
> Kissing with inside lip? Stopping the career [1]
> Of laughter with a sigh?
>   … Is this nothing?
> Why then the world and all that's in't is nothing,
> The covering sky is nothing, Bohemia nothing,
> My wife is nothing, nor nothing have these nothings,
> If this be nothing.
> Camillo: Good my lord, be cured
> Of this diseased opinion, and betimes, [2]
> For 'tis most dangerous.

[1] *course*
[2] *without delay*

A murder is planned

Leontes lashes out furiously at Camillo, declaring him to be a liar. Any loyal courtier with a genuine sense of honour, he claims, would take action to end the queen's illicit affair by killing Polixenes. In fact Camillo, as the king's official cupbearer, is perfectly placed to do just that, by serving their guest with poisoned wine.

Camillo agrees that this would be possible, but he cannot believe that the queen is guilty of adultery. Leontes dismisses his doubts impatiently. He would not put himself through the agony he is currently suffering without good reason, he points out. Finally Camillo backs down, and agrees that Polixenes must be dealt with:

Leontes:	Dost think I am so muddy, so unsettled,
	To appoint myself in this vexation? [1]
	… Give scandal to the blood [2] o'th' prince, my son,
	Who I do think is mine, and love as mine,
	Without ripe moving to't? [3] Would I do this?
	Could man so blench? [4]
Camillo:	I must believe you, sir.
	I do, and will fetch off Bohemia [5] for't …

[1] *so unstable that I would bring this vexation upon myself*
[2] *cast doubt on the parentage*
[3] *without a well founded motive*
[4] *go so far from the truth, make such a mistake*
[5] *remove Polixenes*

There is one condition, says Camillo: when Polixenes has been disposed of, the king must never again suggest that Hermione has behaved dishonourably. Their marriage must be as it was before and, for the sake of their son and the reputation of the kingdom, there must not be the slightest suggestion of infidelity attached to the queen.

Leontes agrees, and confirms that he had come to the same conclusion himself. He agrees, too, that he must continue to treat their guest in a friendly, hospitable manner. After their next meal together, promises Camillo, Polixenes will no longer be a problem. The king is satisfied, but as he leaves he gives Camillo a final warning:

Camillo:	I am his cupbearer.
	If from me he have wholesome beverage,
	Account me not your servant.
Leontes:	This is all.
	Do't, and thou hast the one half of my heart;
	Do't not, thou splitt'st thine own.

A hasty decision

Alone, Camillo's first thought is for the queen and the threat to her reputation. He then contemplates his own appalling predicament: he has agreed to poison Polixenes, the good king of Bohemia, who is surely innocent. Leontes is clearly not in his right mind, and will execute him if he fails in his duty. He has no choice, he decides, but to exile himself from the court of Sicilia.

Polixenes now enters. He has just passed Leontes, and noticed that his friend seemed troubled and withdrawn, and did not even respond to his greeting. Camillo is unwilling to talk directly about the king's behaviour, making Polixenes all the more perplexed, particularly as he himself seems to be involved:

> Camillo: There is a sickness
> Which puts some of us in distemper,[1] but
> I cannot name the disease, and it is caught
> Of you that yet are well.[2]
> Polixenes: How caught of me?
> Make me not sighted like the basilisk.[3]
> I have looked on thousands who have sped the better
> By my regard,[4] but killed none so.

> [1] *makes some of us irrational*
> [2] *from people like yourself who are still well*
> [3] *don't suggest that I'm like the mythical basilisk,*
>   *which could kill people merely by looking at them*
> [4] *who have profited from my glance*

Eventually Camillo reveals the truth: he has been instructed to murder Polixenes. The order has come from Leontes, who is convinced that he has seduced the queen.

Polixenes is bewildered, and shocked that his friend could believe such a thing. Nothing will change Leontes' mind, warns Camillo. He is utterly convinced, and will not listen to reason:

Camillo: … you may as well
            Forbid the sea for to obey the moon
            As or by oath remove or counsel shake
            The fabric of his folly,[1] whose foundation
            Is piled upon his faith[2] and will continue
            The standing of his body.[3]

            [1] *alter his irrational delusion either by swearing oaths*
               or through sensible argument
            [2] *which is based on his absolute conviction*
            [3] *as long as he lives*

The matter is urgent, Camillo declares. Both their lives are in
danger. He offers to help Polixenes and his attendants to leave
Sicilia in secrecy this very night: as a trusted adviser to the king,
Camillo is authorised to use the various hidden gates in the city
walls. In return, he asks if he may join Polixenes' entourage and
travel with him to Bohemia.

Polixenes trusts Camillo's judgement, and willingly goes along
with his proposal. Remaining in Sicilia and confronting Leontes
would be reckless, and might put the queen in peril, despite her
innocence. Leontes' anger, though misguided, is likely to be
deadly:

Polixenes: This jealousy
            Is for a precious creature. As she's rare,[1]
            Must it[2] be great; and, as his person's mighty,
            Must it be violent, and as he does conceive
            He is dishonoured by a man which ever
            Professed to him,[3] why, his revenges must
            In that be made more bitter.

            [1] *wonderful, exquisite*
            [2] *so must his jealous anger*
            [3] *who has always claimed to be his friend*

Camillo immediately sets about organising their departure.

Leontes passes judgement

Unaware of her husband's troubled state of mind, Hermione is with her ladies-in-waiting and her young son Mamillius. The boy is pestering her, and she asks one of her ladies to look after him. He speaks defiantly to his carers:

> *Lady:* Come, my gracious lord,
> Shall I be your playfellow?
> *Mamillius:* No, I'll none of you.[1]
> *Lady:* Why, my sweet lord?
> *Mamillius:* You'll kiss me hard, and speak to me as if
> I were a baby still.
>
> [1] *I won't have anything to do with you*

One of the women mentions that the queen is expecting another child. Mamillius may be choosy about his companions now, she warns, but he will have to fight for his share of attention when the new baby arrives:

> *Lady:* Hark ye,
> The queen, your mother, rounds apace.[1] We shall
> Present our services to a fine new prince
> One of these days, and then you'd wanton with us [2]
> If we would have you.
>
> [1] *is quickly growing fuller*
> [2] *you'll be determined to play with us*

Hermione comes back to her son and tries to settle him down. She asks him to tell a story:

> *Hermione:* Pray you sit by us,
> And tell's a tale.
> *Mamillius:* Merry or sad shall't be?
> *Hermione:* As merry as you will.[1]
> *Mamillius:* A sad tale's best for winter. I have one
> Of sprites [2] and goblins.
>
> [1] *as you like*
> [2] *spirits, ghosts*

> *A sad tale's best for winter.*
>
> *"The phrase 'a winter's tale' referred to gossip, outright lies, or to the kind of trivial fairy story that no one but nursemaids and children would find entertaining ... Shakespeare used the title to challenge the audience. Calling the play 'the winter's tale' distinguished it from the commonplace saying. This is it, the title declares, this is the ultimate fanciful story: how much of it will you believe?"*
>
> John Pitcher, Introduction to the Arden edition of *The Winter's Tale*, 2010

Suddenly Leontes enters, accompanied by a group of courtiers. He has just been informed of the abrupt departure of Polixenes and his attendants, in the company of his own adviser Camillo.

The news has confirmed the king's worst fears. He feels a grim satisfaction that he was correct to mistrust Polixenes, but wishes at the same time that he had never known the truth:

Leontes: How blest am I
In my just censure, in my true opinion![1]
Alack, for lesser knowledge[2] – how accursed
In being so blest.

[1] *in making the right judgement, and condemning Polixenes*
[2] *if only I hadn't realised*

Leontes compares himself to a man who has been poisoned. If a person takes poison unknowingly, he believes, it may have no effect. It is the awareness of taking it that is fatal:

> *Leontes:*   There may be in the cup
> A spider steeped,[1] and one may drink, depart,
> And yet partake no venom, for his knowledge
> Is not infected; but if one present
> Th'abhorred ingredient to his eye, make known
> How he hath drunk,[2] he cracks his gorge, his sides,
> With violent hefts.[3] I have drunk, and seen the spider.

> [1] *a venomous spider submerged*
> [2] *if someone makes the drinker aware of what he has swallowed*
> [3] *he coughs and retches violently*

Leontes is convinced that Polixenes has not only seduced his wife; he intended to murder him as well, and usurp the kingdom of Sicilia. Camillo must have been recruited to Polixenes' cause, and helped him to escape to avoid execution.

Approaching Hermione, Leontes grabs hold of Mamillius and orders his attendants to take the boy away. Hermione, unaware of her husband's state of mind, is stunned. She is even more shocked when Leontes publicly condemns her:

> *Leontes:*   ... let her sport herself
> With that she's big with,[1] for 'tis Polixenes
> Has made thee swell thus.

> [1] *let her play with the child she's carrying now*

Hermione attempts to answer her husband, but he presses ahead with his denunciation, describing her crimes to the assembled lords.

The queen is appalled at the allegations, but she is equally concerned for the king's well-being. Sooner or later he will regret making these false accusations:

> *Leontes:*   I have said
> She's an adulteress, I have said with whom.
> More, she's a traitor, and Camillo is
> A federary with her [1] …
>   … ay, and privy
> To this their late escape. [2]
> *Hermione:*   No, by my life,
> Privy to none of this. How will this grieve you
> When you shall come to clearer knowledge, that
> You thus have published me? [3]

> [1] *she has conspired with Camillo*
> [2] *she was aware of the plan for Camillo and Polixenes
> to leave the country*
> [3] *you have publicly accused me in this way*

Leontes insists that his statements are founded on solid, indisputable evidence. He orders his guards to take her to prison. Anyone who speaks in her defence, he announces threateningly, will be considered guilty of treason.

Hermione calmly addresses the company. She accepts that she must obey the king, but is confident that the present confusion will pass. She asks them not to mistake her self-control for lack of feeling:

> *Hermione:*   There's some ill planet reigns.
> I must be patient till the heavens look
> With an aspect more favourable. Good my lords,
> I am not prone to weeping, as our sex
> Commonly are, the want of which vain dew
> Perchance shall dry your pities; [1] but I have
> That honourable grief lodged here which burns
> Worse than tears drown. [2]

> [1] *the lack of futile tears will perhaps make you less
> sympathetic*
> [2] *which is more painful and deadly than tears*

By now, Hermione's ladies-in-waiting are all weeping. She reassures them that she is doing the right thing, and asks the king to allow them to stay with her and see her through her pregnancy.

Leontes impatiently orders his guards, once more, to take the queen to prison.

Dissent in the palace

When Hermione and her women have been escorted out, the king's advisers, despite his earlier threat, start to voice their concerns. The nobleman Antigonus is one of the first to speak:

> *Lord:* Beseech your highness, call the queen again.[1]
> *Antigonus:* Be certain what you do, sir, lest your justice
> Prove violence,[2] in the which three great ones suffer:
> Yourself, your queen, your son.
> *Lord:*   For her, my lord,
> I dare my life lay down, and will do't, sir,
> Please you t'accept it, that the queen is spotless[3] ...

> [1] *call the queen back*
> [2] *turns out to be destructive*
> [3] *innocent, without fault*

Antigonus, convinced of Hermione's innocence, believes that the king has been deceived by someone with evil intentions. For his part, Leontes is outraged that his followers appear to doubt his word. He knows the truth, he declares angrily, and does not need their advice.

Leontes now announces that he has sent two noblemen, Cleomenes and Dion, to consult the oracle on the island of Delphos, birthplace of the god Apollo. The oracle's judgement will justify his treatment of Hermione and her associates.

This should be enough to satisfy those who refuse to accept the facts of the matter, he tells his courtiers pointedly:

> Leontes: Though I am satisfied,[1] and need no more
> Than what I know, yet shall the oracle
> Give rest to[2] th' minds of others; such as he
> Whose ignorant credulity will not
> Come up to th' truth.[3]
>
> [1] *I am persuaded by the evidence*
> [2] *resolve, put at ease*
> [3] *those whose simple-mindedness prevents them*
>   *from facing up to the truth*

Meanwhile, the queen must remain in prison: now that her co-conspirators Polixenes and Camillo have fled, there is a danger that she may carry out the planned assassination herself.

A new life   II, ii

Paulina, a Sicilian noblewoman married to Antigonus, has come to visit Hermione in prison. The jailer tells her, respectfully, that he has strict orders that no one is to see the queen. However, he agrees to fetch Emilia, one of the queen's companions, as long as he is present at the meeting.

When the jailer brings Emilia in, she reveals some important news:

> Emilia: On[1] her frights and griefs –
> Which never tender lady hath borne greater –
> She is, something before her time, delivered.[2]
> Paulina: A boy?
> Emilia: A daughter, and a goodly babe,
> Lusty, and like to live.[3] The queen receives
> Much comfort in't …
>
> [1] *as well as, on top of*
> [2] *she has given birth, earlier than expected*
> [3] *healthy, and likely to survive*

Paulina believes that the news may change Leontes' attitude to his wife, particularly if he sees the baby. She offers to take the girl into his presence:

> Paulina: If she dares trust me with her little babe,
> I'll show't the king, and undertake to be
> Her advocate to th' loudest.[1] We do not know
> How he may soften at the sight o'th' child.
> The silence often of pure innocence
> Persuades when speaking fails.
>
> [1] *to put Hermione's case as forcefully as possible*

Emilia agrees enthusiastically; the queen herself had already considered such a plan. At this point, however, the jailer intervenes. He explains, apologetically, that he has no authority to allow the baby out of the prison. Paulina overrules him. It is the queen who has been sentenced, not the child:

> Paulina: You need not fear it, sir.
> This child was prisoner to the womb, and is
> By law and process of great Nature thence
> Freed and enfranchised,[1] not a party to[2]
> The anger of the king ...
>
> [1] *has already been set free from its prison, according to the laws of nature*
> [2] *a target of*

Persuaded by Paulina's argument, the jailer agrees that the baby can be released. Paulina promises that she will not allow him to come to any harm as a result of his decision.

Unwelcome visitors

Alone in a room in the palace, Leontes is tormented by lack of sleep and continual anxiety. He will find no peace, he decides, until he has destroyed those who are threatening his crown and his life. Although Polixenes is out of reach, Hermione, the other half of the adulterous couple, is not. Removing her would bring some respite:

> *Leontes:* ... say that she were gone,
> Given to the fire, a moiety[1] of my rest
> Might come to me again.
>
> [1] *a portion, half*

A servant enters the room, bringing news that the king's son Mamillius seems to be recovering. It emerges that the prince's health has suffered since the departure of his mother; the cause, Leontes believes, is the boy's struggle to bear the shame of his mother's behaviour. He orders the servant to leave him and continue to observe his son's progress.

Leontes' dark thoughts quickly return. His revenge on Polixenes and Camillo will have to wait, he tells himself: but the queen must be dealt with as swiftly as possible.

"Despite his age, his kingship, and his fatherhood, emotionally Leontes is stuck at the developmental stage preceding the formation of identity, the stage of undifferentiated oneness with the mother, on which his oneness with Polixenes was modelled. He cannot sustain a relationship with a woman based on the union of his and her separate identities ..."

Coppélia Kahn, *Representing Shakespeare: New Psychoanalytic Essays*, 1980

A sudden commotion at the door disturbs the king. Paulina, carrying the new-born girl, is demanding to be allowed to enter, while the king's servant is struggling to keep her out. Her husband Antigonus, too, is trying to hold her back.

Paulina scolds the king's attendants for failing to stand up to him. They are doing nothing to help him, while her honest message, by contrast, will bring comfort and healing:

Servant: Madam, he hath not slept tonight, commanded
           None should come at him.
Paulina: Not so hot,[1] good sir.
           I come to bring him sleep.
                                      … such as you
           Nourish the cause of his awaking.[2] I
           Do come with words as medicinal as true,
           Honest as either,[3] to purge him of that humour
           That presses him from sleep.[4]

[1] don't treat me so impudently
[2] attendants like you are making his insomnia worse
[3] words that are spoken with good intentions, as well
    as being beneficial and truthful in equal measure
[4] to drive out that agitation that prevents him from
    sleeping

Leontes is irritated at the disturbance, and is particularly displeased that Antigonus is unable to control his wife. When Paulina reveals that she has come from the queen, Leontes angrily orders her to be taken out of the room. She stands her ground, and insists on delivering her message.

When Leontes hears the news of the birth, he loses his temper completely. Paulina too is clearly involved in the treasonous plot against him:

Paulina: The good queen –
For she is good – hath brought you forth a daughter;
                                    [*lays the baby down*]
Here 'tis; commends it to your blessing.

Leontes: Out!
A mankind[1] witch! Hence with her, out o' door;
A most intelligencing bawd.[2]

[1] *unwomanly, unnatural*
[2] *a deceitful go-between gathering information for the lovers, Polixenes and Hermione*

Infuriated by the sight of the child, and exasperated that Paulina has not been removed from his presence, he accuses his courtiers of treachery. He singles out Antigonus, and orders him to get his wife and the baby out of the room:

Leontes: Traitors!
Will you not push her out? Give her the bastard,
Thou dotard;[1] thou art woman-tired, unroosted[2] …

[1] *weak, foolish old man*
[2] *you are henpecked, you have been knocked off your perch*

Paulina orders her husband not to pick up the baby: they must not acknowledge the king's slanderous words. Leontes repeats his assertion and, in his rage, commands that the baby and its mother are to be burnt alive:

Leontes: This brat is none of mine.[1]
It is the issue[2] of Polixenes.
Hence with it, and together with the dam[3]
Commit them to the fire.

[1] *is nothing to do with me*
[2] *offspring, child*
[3] *mother*

Paulina appeals to the lords around her: there is a distinct physical resemblance between the king and the baby, and the girl is clearly his. Leontes threatens her too with death, but she remains calm. The king is dangerously close to becoming a tyrant, she warns him. Leontes is stung by the accusation, and again demands that she be removed:

Paulina:	... this most cruel usage[1] of your queen,
	Not able to produce more accusation
	Than your own weak-hinged fancy,[2] something[3] savours
	Of tyranny, and will ignoble make you,
	Yea, scandalous to the world.
Leontes:	On your allegiance,
	Out of the chamber with her! Were I a tyrant,
	Where were her life?[4] She durst not call me so
	If she did know me one.[5] Away with her!

[1] *treatment*
[2] *deranged imagination*
[3] *somewhat, rather*
[4] *if I were a tyrant, would she still be alive?*
[5] *she would not dare call me a tyrant if I genuinely were one*

Paulina finally leaves, pushing aside the guards who are trying to manhandle her out of the room.

"Leontes seems to be living in a different time-reality from those around him ... Whereas Polixenes and Hermione see a reality embracing past, present and future, Leontes seems trapped in an abrasive now."

Gareth Lloyd Evans, *Shakespeare 1606 – 1616*, 1973

A harsh decree

Leontes turns again to Antigonus. The elderly counsellor has clearly supported his wife Paulina in her attempt to deceive the king, and is therefore guilty of treason himself. His only means of reprieve is to kill the infant himself:

> *Leontes:*   … take it hence,
> And see it instantly consumed[1] with fire.
> Even thou, and none but thou. Take it up straight.[2]
> Within this hour bring me word 'tis done,
> And by good testimony,[3] or I'll seize thy life,
> With what thou else call'st thine.[4]

> [1] *engulfed, destroyed*
> [2] *carry the baby away immediately*
> [3] *with good evidence to prove that you have done it*
> [4] *I'll execute you and confiscate all your possessions*

Antigonus denies having encouraged his wife, and the other courtiers defend him, urging the king to be more lenient. Leontes reluctantly gives way. The child will not be burnt to death, but must instead be abandoned far from Sicilia.

Leontes forces Antigonus to swear, on the king's sword, to carry out the task. As long as this is done, his life, and that of Paulina, will be spared:

> *Leontes:*   We enjoin[1] thee,
> As thou art liegeman[2] to us, that thou carry
> This female bastard hence, and that thou bear it
> To some remote and desert[3] place, quite out
> Of our dominions;[4] and that there thou leave it,
> Without more mercy,[5] to its own protection …

> [1] *command, require*
> [2] *a loyal subject*
> [3] *deserted, uninhabited*
> [4] *far away from my lands*
> [5] *without any further help*

Antigonus vows to carry out the king's command, though he suspects a quick death might be kinder. He carries the baby away sadly, expressing the wish that the king will not suffer as much as he deserves for his cruel decision.

Just after Antigonus' departure, a messenger hurries in. The two officials sent to consult the oracle are on their way to the palace, he reports. They have returned earlier than expected. Leontes takes this as a positive sign; Hermione's guilt was so clear, he believes, that judgement was arrived at without lengthy deliberation. He orders a trial to be arranged so that the verdict can be made public and her sentence carried out without delay:

> Leontes: ... 'tis good speed, foretells
> The great Apollo suddenly will have
> The truth of this appear.[1] Prepare you, lords,
> Summon a session,[2] that we may arraign[3]
> Our most disloyal lady; for, as she hath
> Been publicly accused, so shall she have
> A just and open trial. While she lives
> My heart will be a burden to me.
>
> [1] *must have revealed the truth, through his oracle,*
> *at once*
> [2] *call a meeting of the lords, to act as a court*
> [3] *put on trial*

Word from Delphos

Cleomenes and Dion, the two Sicilian lords dispatched to consult the oracle on the island of Delphos, are on their homeward journey. The visit has made a profound impression on them, and everything about their experience has left them awestruck: the beauty and richness of the island, the solemn, spectacular rituals of the priests, the deafening sound of the oracle itself that emerged from within Apollo's temple.

The two men are unaware of the oracle's judgement on Hermione, which has been written on a scroll and placed inside a sealed container by Apollo's high priest. They are unhappy with Leontes' public condemnation of the queen, and hope that their mission will have proved her innocent:

Dion: If th'event[1] o'th' journey
             Prove as successful to the queen – O, be't so –
             As it hath been to us rare,[2] pleasant, speedy,
             The time is worth the use on't.[3]
Cleomenes: Great Apollo
             Turn all to th' best. These proclamations,
             So forcing faults upon[4] Hermione,
             I little like.

[1] *result, outcome*
[2] *remarkable, wonderful*
[3] *our time will have been well spent*
[4] *attributing crimes to, denouncing*

It is often assumed that Shakespeare had in mind the oracle at Delphi, an important religious site on the Greek mainland. However, his reference to 'the isle of Delphos' is not the result of carelessness or ignorance: this was the name, in Shakespeare's day, of the island of Delos, the birthplace in Greek mythology of the god Apollo.

A temple dedicated to the god was situated on the island. The Greeks believed that, in this temple, Apollo communicated his judgements through his priests and their mysterious, awe-inspiring rituals.

Hermione faces her accuser

The king's lords, advisers and officials are gathered for the trial of Hermione. Leontes announces that he is reluctant to place such an important, much loved figure before the court. Justice must be done, however, and the fact that the session is taking place in public demonstrates his even-handedness:

> *Leontes:*   Let us be cleared
> Of being tyrannous, since we so openly
> Proceed in justice, which shall have due course
> Even to the guilt or the purgation.[1]

> [1] *whether the end result is conviction or acquittal*

Hermione is brought in, accompanied by Paulina and her ladies-in-waiting. An official reads out the charges against the queen: she has committed adultery with Polixenes, has conspired with Camillo to assassinate the king, and has aided the two men in their undercover escape from Sicilia.

The queen is resigned to the fact that she can do nothing more than deny all the charges. If her word is not accepted, she will inevitably be found guilty. She trusts that the truth is known in heaven, and will emerge in time; for the present, however, her life has become so wretched that she would willingly lose it. It is only for the honour of her children that she is determined to clear her name.

Hermione tells her husband that she is bewildered by his accusations. Her behaviour with Polixenes was friendly, but not improper in any way. As for Camillo, she has always regarded him as completely trustworthy, and has no idea why he should have left for Bohemia.

If she loses her life, insists Hermione, it will be because of Leontes' delusions, not for anything that has genuinely happened. Leontes retorts that his imaginings are all too true:

Leontes: You knew of his departure, as you know
What you have underta'en to do in's absence.[1]
Hermione: Sir,
You speak a language that I understand not.
My life stands in the level of your dreams,
Which I'll lay down.[2]
Leontes: Your actions are my dreams.[3]

[1] *you knew about Camillo's departure, and you have
agreed to carry out the planned assassination*
[2] *my life, which I am about to give up, is the target of
your unhealthy imagination*
[3] *it is your corrupt actions that haunt my mind*

Hermione declares, once again, that she is not afraid of death, so there is no need to threaten her. The inexplicable loss of her husband's love has made life unbearable:

Hermione: Sir, spare your threats.
The bug which you would fright me with I seek.[1]
To me can life be no commodity;[2]
The crown and comfort of my life, your favour,
I do give[3] lost, for I do feel it gone
But know not how it went.

[1] *the fate with which you are trying to scare me is
exactly what I am looking for*
[2] *life can hold no value*
[3] *consider*

On top of this, she has been denied access to her son, and has had her new-born daughter snatched away. Her reputation has been tainted and, having barely recovered from childbirth, she has now been forced to appear before a court on fictitious charges. Since there is no one to speak in her defence, she calls on the court to reveal the judgement of the god Apollo, as revealed through his oracle.

The spectacle of a queen on trial would have presented a powerful image to audiences of Shakespeare's time. Within living memory, Mary Queen of Scots, cousin of Queen Elizabeth I, had been tried for treason and executed. The scene would have brought to mind, too, the notorious trial in 1536 of Elizabeth's mother, Anne Boleyn, on charges of adultery, incest and treason.

The emphasis on Hermione's unfaithfulness might also suggest the proceedings of a church court. Although these courts dealt with a range of religious and moral issues, the high proportion of cases involving fornication, adultery, and illegitimate births earned them the nickname 'bawdy courts':

"To a Shakespearean audience, the trial of Queen Hermione for adultery would at one and the same time have evoked a high-level treason trial and a mundane bawdy court case."

Jonathan Bate, *Soul of the Age*, 2009

A double tragedy

Cleomenes and Dion, newly returned from Delphos, now enter the courtroom. They give their solemn oath that they have travelled to the temple of Apollo and brought back the word of the oracle, as yet unread, in a sealed container.

Leontes orders the court official to break the seal and read the scroll. The message from the oracle is brief, concise, and unambiguous:

Hermione is chaste, Polixenes blameless, Camillo a true subject, Leontes a jealous tyrant, his innocent babe truly begotten ...

The final statement, however, is more enigmatic:

> ... *the king shall live without an heir if that which is lost be not found.*

There is uproar in the courtroom as the assembled lords cry out, overjoyed at the verdict. Leontes, on the other hand, immediately dismisses the judgement, and orders the court to continue with the trial.

At this point a servant rushes in, bringing terrible news. Mamillius, the young prince, already in uncertain health since the imprisonment of his mother, has died. Leontes is devastated, realising in an instant how impetuous and foolish he has been. The oracle spoke the truth, and his blasphemy in rejecting it has been punished:

Leontes: Apollo's angry, and the heavens themselves
Do strike at my injustice.

Amidst the tumult and consternation, Hermione faints to the floor. Paulina cries out, convinced that the news of her son's death has killed her. Leontes tries to reassure Paulina that the queen will recover, and she is carried away, still unconscious, for treatment.

Leontes now addresses the heavens directly, confessing his offences and vowing to make amends:

Leontes: Apollo, pardon
My great profaneness[1] 'gainst thine oracle.
I'll reconcile me to Polixcnes,
New woo my queen,[2] recall the good Camillo,
Whom I proclaim a man of truth ...

[1] *blasphemy, irreverence*
[2] *renew my loving bond with Hermione*

Leontes recalls his previous desire to poison Polixenes, and his attempt to enlist Camillo's assistance. He now sees that Camillo was right to reveal the plot, even though this meant sacrificing the grandeur of his own life in the Sicilian court. He reflects on the stark contrast between Camillo's honourable conduct and his own vindictiveness:

> Leontes: How he glisters
> Through my rust![1] And how his piety
> Does my deeds make the blacker!
>
> [1] *shines through the corruption that I tried to impose*
>   *on his virtue*

Paulina now returns, distraught. Unable to contain her fury, she harangues the king relentlessly. He is responsible for yet another dreadful event, and no expressions of remorse can ever atone for it:

> Paulina: The queen, the queen,
> The sweetest, dearest creature's dead, and vengeance for't
> Not dropped down yet.[1]
> Lord: The higher powers forbid!
> Paulina: I say she's dead – I'll swear't. If word nor oath
> Prevail not,[2] go and see. If you can bring
> Tincture or lustre in her lip, her eye,
> Heat outwardly or breath within, I'll serve you
> As I would do the gods. But O thou tyrant,
> Do not repent these things, for they are heavier
> Than all thy woes can stir.[3]
>
> [1] *has not yet come down from the heavens*
> [2] *if you will not take my word for it*
> [3] *however much you repent, it will not lessen the gravity*
>   *of these crimes*

The king is condemned to a life of perpetual despair, declares Paulina, and nothing will ever induce the gods to look mercifully on him.

Leontes meekly accepts Paulina's verbal onslaught, but the king's attendants reprimand her for her lack of respect. Calming down, she apologises for her outburst. She can see that the king is tormented by his guilt. Encouraging him to suffer further will do nothing to bring back the queen:

> Paulina: Alas, I have showed too much
> The rashness of a woman. He is touched
> To th' noble heart. What's gone and what's past help
> Should be past grief.

Paulina promises to speak no more of the king's misdeeds. At the same time, however, she mentions her husband Antigonus. He is now on his mission, on the king's orders, to take Hermione's new-born baby to a remote, barren place. Paulina fears he may not survive:

> Paulina: ... Sir, royal sir, forgive a foolish woman.
> The love I bore[1] your queen – lo, fool again![2]
> I'll speak of her no more, nor of your children.
> I'll not remember[3] you of my own lord,
> Who is lost too. Take your patience to you,[4]
> And I'll say nothing.
>
> [1] *felt for*
> [2] *I'm being foolish again, mentioning Hermione*
> [3] *remind*
> [4] *arm yourself with patience*

Paulina need not ask for forgiveness, says Leontes; he deserves every word of her criticism, and does not wish to escape from his grief. In fact, he aims to spend the rest of his life mourning the deaths that he has brought about:

> *Leontes:*   Prithee bring me
> To the dead bodies of my queen and son.
> One grave shall be for both. Upon them shall
> The causes of their death appear, unto
> Our shame perpetual.[1] Once a day I'll visit
> The chapel where they lie, and tears shed there
> Shall be my recreation.[2]

[1] *as an everlasting source of shame to me*
[2] *will be my only occupation; I will have no other pastime*

"Mamillius is the focus of the creative life of the court, the centre of loving attention ... For Leontes he is a living image of his own life. His death strikes in turn at the root of the society he lives in, causing its final disintegration ... The community of love which he bound together falls apart as he dies."

Terry Eagleton, *Shakespeare and Society*, 1970

Antigonus completes his mission

Antigonus, carrying the baby girl rejected by the king, has sailed away from Sicilia and landed on a foreign shore. The mariner who has guided him there confirms that the wild, uninhabited place where their ship has moored is Bohemia. He is anxious to leave as soon as possible; the skies are threatening, and a storm is on its way.

The mariner suspects that the gods disapprove of the cruel act that his passenger has promised to carry out. Antigonus asks him to return to their vessel, assuring him that he will follow shortly. With a warning that the area is notorious for dangerous beasts of prey, the mariner leaves, glad to get away from such hostile surroundings.

Antigonus sets off to find a suitable place to abandon the infant. He reveals that, although he does not believe in ghosts, the dead Hermione appeared to him in his cabin last night. The figure, dressed in pure white robes, instructed him to leave the baby in Bohemia, and to name it Perdita. She warned that, although he was not acting out of choice, he would suffer for the task he had undertaken.

He remembers every word uttered by the apparition:

Antigonus: 'Good Antigonus,
　　　　　… Places remote enough are in Bohemia;
　　　　　There weep, and leave it crying; and for[1] the babe
　　　　　Is counted lost for ever, Perdita[2]
　　　　　I prithee call't. For this ungentle business
　　　　　Put on thee by my lord,[3] thou ne'er shalt see
　　　　　Thy wife Paulina more.' And so, with shrieks,
　　　　　She melted into air.

　　　[1] *since*
　　　[2] *in Latin, 'the lost girl'*
　　　[3] *as a result of this unkind deed imposed on you by*
　　　　my husband

Antigonus is sure that this was nothing more than a dream, but despite himself he has followed the instruction to go ashore at Bohemia. Perhaps the king was right, he muses, and the child is not his; perhaps the gods, with this dream, have made sure that she is left to live or die in the land of her true father, Polixenes?

Without further delay, Antigonus finds a place to lay the baby. Next to her he leaves a box containing a letter that he has written in case anyone should find her, along with enough gold to pay for her upbringing. The predicted storm now arrives, and Antigonus hurries towards his ship. Suddenly he hears the sound of horns and dogs: a hunt is in progress, and a bear has been flushed out. It heads directly for Antigonus, who runs for his life.

Exit, pursued by a bear.

The Globe Theatre, owned by Shakespeare's acting company, was situated just outside the City of London, beyond the control of the city authorities. The area was home to many taverns and brothels, as well as a number of theatres. Another attraction was the Bear Garden, where bears, usually chained to a post, would be pitted against ferocious dogs, or taunted by men with whips. Although the activity seems barbaric now, bear-baiting was hugely popular in Shakespeare's day; Queen Elizabeth, for example, was very keen on it, as had been her father, King Henry VIII. Some bears became famous for their resilience and courage, and were given nicknames by regular patrons.

It has been suggested that Antigonus would have been chased off the Globe stage by a real bear, borrowed from the nearby Bear Garden, but this is almost certainly false:

"The Winter's Tale contains Shakespeare's best-known stage direction: 'Exit, pursued by a bear.' It is tempting to speculate that the famous Sackerson or his colleague Henry Hunks from the nearby Bear Garden might have been incorporated into the cast, but this is highly unlikely. These were fearsome animals, capable of killing anyone who strayed into their path ..."

Nicholas Fogg, *Hidden Shakespeare*, 2013

Mixed fortunes

Out in the Bohemian wilderness, a shepherd is wandering anxiously through the storm. He is annoyed at the youths who have decided to go out hunting in this weather: they have scared away two of his valuable sheep. He takes a dim view of young men in general:

> Shepherd: I would there were no age between ten and three-and-twenty, or that youth would sleep out the rest;[1] for there is nothing in the between but getting wenches with child,[2] wronging the ancientry,[3] stealing, fighting ...
>
> [1] *spend the intervening years asleep*
> [2] *getting young women pregnant*
> [3] *being disrespectful to their elders*

Suddenly the shepherd comes across a bundle on the ground. He realises, to his astonishment, that it is a baby. No doubt it is the product of an illicit affair, he reflects: and judging from the fine material in which it is wrapped, the mother was probably a waiting-woman in a wealthy household.

The shepherd is keen to show the discovery to his son, who has just appeared. The young man, however, is in a state of terrible agitation. He has just seen two dreadful sights. Out on the rough seas, a ship is being tossed around violently, and its occupants thrown into the churning waters; while on land, he has witnessed a man being torn apart by a bear.

The young man, a clownish country bumpkin, slips unintentionally into comedy as he describes the heart-rending incidents:

> Clown: ... how the poor souls roared, and the sea mocked them, and how the poor gentleman roared, and the bear mocked him, both roaring louder than the sea or weather.
> Shepherd: Name of mercy, when was this, boy?
> Clown: Now, now. I have not winked since I saw these sights. The men are not yet cold under the water, nor the bear half dined on the gentleman ...

The shepherd is shocked by the news, but reveals that he, by contrast, has had a more hopeful encounter:

Shepherd: Heavy[1] matters, heavy matters. But look thee here,
boy. Now bless thyself;[2] thou met'st with[3] things
dying, I with things newborn.

[1] *distressing, serious*
[2] *consider yourself fortunate*
[3] *came across, witnessed*

The shepherd shows his son the baby he has found. Noticing that there is a box next to it, the shepherd mentions that he was once told by a fortune-teller that the fairies would make him rich. When the box is opened, the prediction is proved true; there is enough gold in it to make him wealthy for the rest of his life.

They must not tell anyone about the money, the shepherd tells his son. He intends to take it home straight away, along with the baby; the lost sheep can take care of themselves. The young man decides that the victim of the bear must be attended to first:

Clown: Go you the next way[1] with your findings. I'll go see
if the bear be gone from the gentleman, and how much
he hath eaten. They are never curst but when they are
hungry.[2] If there be any of him left, I'll bury it.

[1] *take the shortest way home*
[2] *they are only aggressive when they are hungry*

The shepherd is pleased with his son's thoughtfulness. Now that they are rich, he declares, they will be able to carry out many such acts of kindness:

Shepherd: 'Tis a lucky day, boy, and we'll do good deeds on't.[1]

[1] *as a result of this day*

Time passes

The winged figure of Time now appears on stage carrying, as is the tradition, an hourglass. He asks the audience to imagine that sixteen years have passed.

The events of these past years need not concern us: we might imagine, suggests Time, that we have had a long sleep and woken up sixteen years later. The action of the play will now start afresh, he announces, turning his hourglass upside down:

> *Time:*   Your patience this allowing,[1]
> I turn my glass, and give my scene such growing
> As you had slept between.[2]
>
> [1] *if you'll be patient enough to believe in my powers*
> [2] *make the plot develop so suddenly that you'll think
> you have slept through the intervening time*

For the present, we are leaving the Sicilian king Leontes, who in his grief has shut himself away from society. Instead, says Time, the scene moves to the court of Bohemia. He reminds us that the king, Polixenes, has a son named Florizel: and we must not forget Perdita, now a shepherd's daughter, who is growing into a beautiful woman. Their stories will follow, promises Time.

"Time has his traditional hourglass with him, which he turns over mid-way through his speech. This means that the first half of the play is over and the second can begin. The gesture, conventional enough to modern eyes, alerted early audiences to something unusual. In the second 'hour' of the play, they would see the social order turned upside down ..."

John Pitcher, Introduction to the Arden edition of *The Winter's Tale*, 2010

Time asks us once more to accept his words in good faith, as long as the action of the play has pleased us so far. If, on the other hand, we feel that our time has been wasted, Time himself hopes that it will never happen again:

Time: Of this allow,[1]
        If ever you have spent time worse ere now;
        If never, yet [2] that Time himself doth say
        He wishes earnestly you never may.

        [1] believe what I say
        [2] if you have never had a worse time, still take my
            word for it

A wayward son   IV, ii

Since his flight from Sicilia many years ago, Camillo has become an invaluable adviser at the court of king Polixenes. As he grows older, however, the nobleman yearns more and more to return to his homeland. The king is torn; he hates to refuse his friend anything, but Camillo has become an essential asset to the kingdom of Bohemia.

Camillo mentions that Leontes is still grieving over his impetuous, destructive actions that have caused so much distress. Camillo's return would be a great comfort to the Sicilian king:

Polixenes: I pray thee, good Camillo, be no more importunate.[1]
            'Tis a sickness denying thee anything, a death to grant
            this.[2]
Camillo: It is fifteen years since I saw my country. Though I
            have for the most part been aired abroad,[3] I desire to
            lay my bones there. Besides, the penitent king, my
            master, hath sent for me, to whose feeling sorrows I
            might be some allay[4] ...

        [1] please don't keep asking for my permission
        [2] denying you anything is painful, but agreeing to let
            you leave would be fatal
        [3] although I have spent most of my life abroad
        [4] whose profound sadness I may be able to alleviate

Polixenes is unsettled by the mention of Sicilia and its king. The memory of the deaths of queen Hermione and her two children is still painful. His thoughts turn to his own son, Florizel, whose recent behaviour has been troublesome.

Camillo comments that he has not seen the prince for three days: he seems to be neglecting his royal duties. The king agrees, and reveals that he knows where the young man is spending his time:

Polixenes: ... I have eyes under my service which look upon
  his removedness,[1] from whom I have this intelligence:
  that he is seldom from[2] the house of a most homely
  shepherd, a man, they say, that from very nothing, and
  beyond the imagination of his neighbours, is grown into
  an unspeakable estate.[3]

Camillo: I have heard, sir, of such a man, who hath a daughter of
  most rare note.[4]

  [1] *spies who check on his whereabouts when he is not
  at court*
  [2] *away from*
  [3] *has become indescribably rich, to the bewilderment
  of his neighbours*
  [4] *of remarkable merit*

The shepherd's daughter is widely admired, remarks Camillo; it is hard to believe that she is from such humble origins. Polixenes, however, is concerned that the prince should be spending so much time with such a low-born girl. He intends to visit the shepherd, in disguise, and find out more.

The king asks Camillo to abandon his thoughts of returning to Sicilia and, instead, help him to investigate Florizel's misconduct.

Easy pickings

A shabbily dressed vagabond is strolling along a country lane in Bohemia, singing. In his song, he boasts of thieving and debauchery. He was once a servant to prince Florizel, he remarks regretfully, but has since gone down in the world.

He specialises in stealing linen sheets that have been hung out to dry, but will pilfer whatever is available: this way of life runs in the family, he claims. However, his ill-gotten gains are quickly spent, and his precarious existence has left him in rags:

> *Autolycus:* My father named me Autolycus,[1] who being, as I am, littered under Mercury,[2] was likewise a snapper-up of unconsidered trifles.[3] With die and drab I purchased this caparison[4] ...

> [1] *in Greek, 'the lone wolf'*
> [2] *born under the influence of Mercury, the god of trickery and deception*
> [3] *someone who steals small items when the owner isn't paying attention*
> [4] *my money has gone on gambling and prostitutes, leaving me in these tattered clothes*

Fearful of punishment, Autolycus avoids the highways, preferring to target the unsophisticated folk to be found on rural byways. He cannot believe his luck when he sees just such a victim, a country bumpkin on his way to market, coming towards him.

The man is the shepherd's simple-minded son. A feast is soon to take place to celebrate the summertime sheep-shearing, and he has been tasked by his young sister Perdita with buying supplies. He is looking at her shopping list and attempting, unsuccessfully, to calculate how much he needs to spend:

> *Clown:* ... Fifteen hundred shorn, what comes the wool to?[1]
> *Autolycus:* If the springe hold, the cock's mine.[2]
> *Clown:* I cannot do't without counters. Let me see, what am I to buy for our sheep-shearing feast? Three pound of

sugar, five pound of currants, rice – what will this
sister of mine do with rice? But my father hath made
her mistress of the feast, and she lays it on.[3]

[1] *if we shear fifteen hundred sheep, how much will
   we get for the wool?*
[2] *if the snare works, I'll catch this woodcock*
[3] *she's sparing no expense*

Fifteen hundred shorn, what comes the wool to?

Shakespeare almost certainly had first-hand experience of the
wool trade in his early years. Wool was a valuable commodity;
the market was controlled by the government, and wool could
only be traded by licensed dealers. Shakespeare's father John,
though often referred to as a glover, was heavily involved in
'brogging', or unlicensed wool dealing. His shady business
dealings got him into trouble on more than one occasion:

*"The Elizabethan government employed a network of
informers, spies and bounty hunters, who pried into every
aspect of people's business affairs ... when Shakespeare was
eight, John came before the courts on two charges of illegal
wool dealing. The two purchases were of a couple of tons of
wool, purchased for £210 in cash at a time when a good house
cost £60 ... this was a very competitive business of high risk
and fast profit in an uncertain economic climate."*

Michael Wood, *In Search of Shakespeare*, 2005

When Shakespeare was twelve, his father's finances
deteriorated drastically, through a combination of punitive
fines, bad debts and a growing crisis in the wool industry.
Much of the family's property and land had to be sold or
mortgaged. At fourteen, William was taken out of school,
probably to help in his father's glovemaking business. It was
to be another twenty years before the family's fortunes were
restored, largely with the help of their son William and his
flourishing career in the world of London theatre.

Autolycus throws himself to the ground melodramatically. He has been robbed and beaten, he cries: his attacker has even stolen his clothes, leaving him with the rags he is now wearing.

The shepherd's son helps him to his feet sympathetically, and Autolycus, grimacing and groaning with pain, takes the opportunity to pick his pocket. He hastily refuses the offer of money as, a moment later, the young man starts to reach into the pocket where his purse had been.

Pressed for a description of his assailant, Autolycus says that it was someone he knows well, a man who used to serve prince Florizel. The shepherd's son confirms that the man is a notorious thief, but a cowardly one:

> Clown: ... He haunts wakes,[1] fairs and bear-baitings.
> Autolycus: Very true, sir. He, sir, he. That's the rogue that put me
>   into this apparel.[2]
> Clown: Not a more cowardly rogue in all Bohemia. If you had
>   but looked big and spit at him, he'd have run.
> Autolycus: I must confess to you, sir, I am no fighter. I am false
>   of heart that way, and that he knew, I warrant him.[3]

> [1] *feasts, festivals*
> [2] *who forced me to wear these clothes*
> [3] *I guarantee it, I can speak for him*

Autolycus, now recovered, hurriedly takes his leave before his victim discovers his loss. The mention of the sheep-shearing feast has aroused his interest, and he is determined to make the most of the opportunity:

> Autolycus: I'll be with you at your sheep-shearing, too. If I make
>   not this cheat bring out another[1] and the shearers prove
>   sheep,[2] let me be unrolled[3] and my name put in the
>   book of virtue.

> [1] *if I can't make this piece of trickery lead on to another*
> [2] *show the shearers to be as easily deceived as their sheep*
> [3] *let me be removed from the book of villains*

Young love

The day of the sheep-shearing feast has arrived, and the guests are about to appear at the shepherd's cottage. Prince Florizel, dressed as a country dweller, is already present. He is immersed in conversation with his sweetheart, the shepherd's daughter Perdita. She is wearing festive clothes and garlands of flowers for the occasion, but feels self-conscious in her unfamiliar costume.

Florizel assures her that her appearance suits the event perfectly, but she remains uneasy. Both of them, in different ways, have overstepped the mark:

> *Florizel:* These your unusual weeds[1] to each part of you
> Does give a life; no shepherdess, but Flora
> Peering in April's front.[2] This your sheep-shearing
> Is as a meeting of the petty[3] gods,
> And you the queen on't.
>
> *Perdita:* ... Your high self,
> The gracious mark o'th' land,[4] you have obscured
> With a swain's wearing,[5] and me, poor lowly maid,
> Most goddess-like pranked up.[6]

> [1] *unfamiliar garments*
> [2] *the goddess of flowers and spring, making her appearance in early April*
> [3] *minor, lesser*
> [4] *the object, as prince, of the whole kingdom's attention*
> [5] *a country dweller's clothes*
> [6] *adorned, dressed up*

Perdita is acutely aware of the difference in their status. She is sure that Florizel's father, the king, will oppose his son's engagement to a shepherd's daughter when he discovers the truth. He would be appalled, if he could see them now, to find the prince in his rough, rustic garments.

Florizel assures Perdita that his father's attitude will not make the slightest difference to his love for her. If necessary, he will cut himself off completely from the king. He urges her to be cheerful and to think of the marriage that, they have both agreed, will soon take place:

Florizel: ... I prithee darken not
The mirth o'th' feast – or[1] I'll be thine, my fair,
Or not my father's. For I cannot be
Mine own, nor anything to any, if
I be not thine. To this I am most constant,
Though[2] destiny say no.
... Lift up your countenance as[3] it were the day
Of celebration of that nuptial which
We two have sworn shall come.

[1] *either*
[2] *even if*
[3] *as if*

Perdita hopes fervently that fortune will favour the two of them. Florizel encourages her to put on a brave face: the guests are approaching.

"The Winter's Tale *may be called the gentlest of Shakespeare's plays. It is done with a tenderer hand than the other works."*

John Masefield, *William Shakespeare*, 1911

Flowers for the guests

The old shepherd hurries in, scolding Perdita for neglecting their guests. He remembers how his wife, now dead, used to be the life and soul of the of the annual sheep-shearing party:

Shepherd: Fie, daughter, when my old wife lived, upon
This day she was both pantler,[1] butler, cook;
Both dame and servant, welcomed all, served all,
Would sing her song and dance her turn, now here
At upper end o'th' table, now i'th' middle ...
You are retired[2]
As if you were a feasted one[3] and not
The hostess of the meeting.

[1] servant in charge of the food
[2] reticent, restrained
[3] guest

Among the various shepherds, shepherdesses and farmhands who have come to the cottage are two strangers. The old shepherd encourages his daughter to welcome them to the gathering, not realising that the two men are the king and his adviser in disguise.

Perdita dutifully addresses the strangers, and hands them flowers. Polixenes remarks ironically that they are flowers that thrive in winter:

Perdita: Reverend sirs,
For you there's rosemary and rue; these keep
Seeming and savour[1] all the winter long.
Grace and remembrance be to you both,
And welcome to our shearing.
Polixenes: Shepherdess,
A fair one are you. Well you fit our ages
With flowers of winter.

[1] their appearance and their fragrance

> *"The intervention of a sixteen-year gap in the action has a curious double effect. In one sense it represents an astonishingly swift passage of time, a wild acceleration of the hectic pace of the first three acts; in another and more important sense, however, it introduces a new temporal framework of larger and more extended rhythms: the minutes, hours, days, and months of Leontes' fevered world are suddenly replaced by the more spacious and deliberate movement of the seasons of the year and the succession of human generations."*
>
> David Young, *The Heart's Forest*, 1972

There are flowers that are at their best in autumn, admits Perdita, but she disapproves of them, and has none for her guests. She believes that their gaudy colours and patterns are the result of human interference with nature:

Perdita:	Sir, the year growing ancient,
	Not yet on summer's death, nor on the birth
	Of trembling winter, the fairest flowers o'th' season
	Are our carnations and streaked gillyvors,[1]
	Which some call Nature's bastards; of that kind
	Our rustic garden's barren, and I care not
	To get slips of them.[2]
Polixenes:	Wherefore,[3] gentle maiden,
	Do you neglect them?
Perdita:	For I have heard it said
	There is an art which in their piedness shares
	With great creating Nature.[4]

[1] *many-coloured gillyflowers*
[2] *to take cuttings to plant in our garden*
[3] *why*
[4] *there is an artificial method of creating their patterned appearance which involves meddling with nature*

Polixenes is intrigued by the strength of the young woman's feelings, but he disagrees with her. Human ability to influence nature is itself part of the natural order of things:

Polixenes: You see, sweet maid, we marry
A gentler scion to the wildest stock,[1]
And make conceive a bark of baser kind
By bud of nobler race.[2] This is an art
Which does mend Nature – change it rather – but
The art itself is Nature.[3]

[1] *we graft a cutting from a superior, cultivated specimen onto the stem of a wild plant*
[2] *make the bark of a common, wild tree produce a shoot of higher quality*
[3] *the ability to change nature in this way is natural*

Perdita continues to resist the idea of growing showy, artificially bred flowers in her garden. To illustrate her point, she mentions her sweetheart, Florizel: although Perdita does not use cosmetics to beautify herself, she would hate to think that, if she did, it would be the only reason that he found her attractive.

To settle the discussion, Perdita chooses some flowers which she trusts will please her two guests:

Perdita: Here's flowers for you:
Hot[1] lavender, mints, savory, marjoram,
The marigold, that goes to bed wi'th' sun,
And with him rises, weeping.[2] These are flowers
Of middle summer, and I think they are given
To men of middle age. You're very welcome.

[1] *sun-loving; potent, pungent*
[2] *that closes at sunset and opens, wet with dew, at sunrise*

A watchful eye

Leaving the two strangers, Perdita starts handing out flowers to the other guests. She regrets that has no flowers of early spring to match the youth and promise of her beloved, and imagines covering him extravagantly with violets and primroses. She is surprised at her own boldness; the fact that she is dressed as the queen of the sheep-shearing has gone to her head, she suspects. Florizel, however, is delighted. She can do no wrong in his eyes:

> *Perdita:* Methinks I play as I have seen them do
> In Whitsun pastorals;[1] sure this robe of mine
> Does change my disposition.[2]
> *Florizel:*   What you do
> Still betters what is done.[3]

> [1] *rural springtime festivals*
> [2] *mood, temperament*
> [3] *whatever you do, you always make your actions seem special*

> *... I play as I have seen them do*
> *In Whitsun pastorals ...*

By 1610, when *The Winter's Tale* was written, the Church of England had been independent from Rome for over fifty years. Many old Catholic festivals and traditions persisted, however, as well as traces of older pre-Christian customs:

"Up and down the country, the old medieval calendar of Catholic saints' days merged with half-forgotten pagan rituals to create an almanac of continuous entertainment, from pancake flipping in the streets on Shrove Tuesday to the rites of May Day ... Whitsuntide or Pentecost, the seventh Sunday after Easter, was an excuse for dancing on the village green, greyhound racing and wrestling contests, plus traditional folk-plays."

Catharine Arnold, *Globe: Life in Shakespeare's London*, 2015

The dancing is about to start, and Florizel leads his partner away. The disguised king and his companion are fascinated by the shepherd's daughter, with her gracious manner and fair complexion:

Polixenes: This is the prettiest low-born lass that ever
Ran on the greensward.[1] Nothing she does or seems
But smacks of [2] something greater than herself,
Too noble for this place.
Camillo: He tells her something
That makes her blood look out.[3] Good sooth, she is
The queen of curds and cream.

[1] *grass, meadow*
[2] *everything about her hints at*
[3] *something that has made her blush*

The musicians strike up a tune. Florizel, Perdita and the young shepherds and shepherdesses join in the dance. Meanwhile, the king questions the old shepherd about his daughter and her dancing-partner.

It becomes clear that Florizel has used an assumed name, Doricles, when visiting the cottage: and although Perdita knows that he is the king's son, he has hidden his true identity from her father, pretending instead to be a wealthy landowner. The old shepherd has noticed, with approval, that they are very much in love:

Polixenes: Pray, good shepherd, what fair swain[1] is this
Which dances with your daughter?
Shepherd: They call him Doricles, and boasts himself
To have a worthy feeding[2] ...
                                He says he loves my daughter;
I think so, too, for never gazed the moon
Upon the water as he'll stand and read,
As 'twere, my daughter's eyes; and, to be plain,
I think there is not half a kiss to choose
Who loves another best.

[1] *young man, admirer*
[2] *he claims to possess valuable pasturelands*

The shepherd is very proud of his daughter, he confides to the strangers. Although he keeps his own wealth a secret, he hints that Perdita's future husband will receive a substantial sum of money as her dowry:

> Polixenes: She dances featly.[1]
> Shepherd: So she does anything, though I report it
>   That should be silent.[2] If young Doricles
>   Do light upon her,[3] she shall bring him that
>   Which he not dreams of.
>
> [1] gracefully, elegantly
> [2] though, as her father, I shouldn't say so myself
> [3] is lucky enough to marry her

A tempting array

A servant interrupts the festivities to announce that a pedlar has just arrived, selling an amazing variety of goods and song-sheets. The shepherd's son, who loves singing, is delighted. The servant naively assures him that the songs, unlike most popular ballads, are suitable for everyone, although the examples he gives suggest otherwise:

> Clown: I love a ballad but even too well, if it be doleful matter
>   merrily set down, or a very pleasant thing indeed and
>   sung lamentably.
> Servant: He hath songs for man or woman of all sizes ... He has
>   the prettiest love songs for maids, so without bawdry,[1]
>   which is strange,[2] with such delicate burdens[3] of dildos
>   and fadings,[4] 'jump her and thump her'...
>
> [1] inoffensive, without obscenity
> [2] unusual
> [3] choruses, refrains
> [4] sighings, moanings

The shepherd's son tells the servant to let the man in. His sister Perdita warns the servant that the visitor had better mind his language.

Autolycus enters, carrying his pack of fancy goods. He is in disguise, and the shepherd's son fails to recognise the man who recently stole his purse. The pedlar sings enthusiastically about the variety and quality of his wares:

Autolycus: Lawn[1] as white as driven snow,
Cypress[2] black as e'er was crow,
Gloves as sweet as damask roses,
Masks for faces and for noses;
Bugle-bracelet,[3] necklace-amber,
Perfume for a lady's chamber ...

[1] *linen or fine cotton*
[2] *fine muslin, gauze*
[3] *a bracelet made of black glass beads*

The shepherd's son has promised to buy some luxuries for his sweetheart, the shepherdess Mopsa. He mentions that he was robbed not long ago, and Autolycus agrees that there are plenty of thieves on the roads.

The pedlar's copious supply of printed songs attracts his customers' attention. Mopsa is particularly keen on those that recount true stories:

Clown: What hast here? Ballads?
Mopsa: Pray now, buy some. I love a ballad in print, a-life,[1] for then we are sure they are true.
Autolycus: Here's one to a very doleful tune, how a usurer's[2] wife was brought to bed of[3] twenty money-bags at a burden[4] ...
Mopsa: Is it true, think you?
Autolycus: Very true, and but a month old.

[1] *on my life*
[2] *moneylender, loan shark*
[3] *gave birth to*
[4] *a single delivery*

The young shepherds eventually find a ballad whose tune they already know, and, along with Autolycus, they start singing raucously. Noticing that his father is deep in conversation with a guest, the shepherd's son leads the singers away, promising to buy ballads and presents for his friends.

Just as the scene has calmed down, the servant comes in again. A troupe of twelve farm workers clad in animal skins has arrived, keen to dance for the gathering. The old shepherd wants to turn them away; there has been enough commotion already. Polixenes, however, is curious to see the rustic performers, and the shepherd reluctantly agrees. The musicians strike up again, the farmhands enter, and the dancing begins.

An abrupt end

Polixenes has decided that it is time to end the relationship between his son and the shepherd girl. Still in disguise, he addresses Florizel. He has noticed that the young man has not bought anything for his sweetheart; when he was young himself, he claims, he would have spared no expense for his true love.

Florizel replies earnestly that the pedlar's goods are of no interest to either of them:

Florizel: Old sir, I know
            She prizes not such trifles as these are.
            The gifts she looks[1] from me are packed and locked
            Up in my heart, which I have given already,
            But not delivered.[2]

[1] *seeks, wants*
[2] *already promised, but not yet given in marriage*

Prompted by Polixenes, Florizel gives a lengthy, impassioned declaration of his love for Perdita:

Florizel: … were I the fairest youth
            That ever made eye swerve,[1] had force and knowledge
            More than was ever man's, I would not prize them
            Without her love …

[1] *attracted attention, turned heads*

The shepherd asks Perdita if she feels the same way. Her reply, though modest, pleases him, and he proposes a formal engagement. He hints, again, that she will bring unexpected wealth to the marriage:

Shepherd: But, my daughter,
            Say you the like[1] to him?
Perdita: I cannot speak
            So well, nothing so well, no, nor mean better.
            By th' pattern of mine own thoughts I cut out
            The purity of his.[2]
Shepherd: Take hands, a bargain;
            And, friends unknown,[3] you shall bear witness to't.
            I give my daughter to him, and will make
            Her portion equal his.[4]

[1] *the same*
[2] *I can judge the purity of his emotions as they match
    mine exactly*
[3] *Polixenes and Camillo*
[4] *the dowry she brings will be equal to the amount he
    already possesses*

Florizel is not concerned about any money Perdita may have; he wants her for herself and her virtues. Besides, he hints, he will one day possess more than the humble shepherd can imagine. The fact that he is the son of a king, and heir to the throne of Bohemia, is a secret he has shared with no one but Perdita, so he can say no more:

Florizel: One being dead,[1]
I shall have more than you can dream of yet,
Enough then for your wonder.[2] But come on,
Contract us[3] 'fore these witnesses.

[1] *when a particular person dies*
[2] *my riches will then be enough to amaze you*
[3] *give your formal consent to our marriage*

At this point Polixenes interrupts the proceedings. He asks, calmly, whether the young man's father has been told of his intention to marry the shepherd girl. When Florizel states bluntly that he has not, Polixenes persists. Perhaps the man in question is too old and feeble to take an interest in his son's affairs, he suggests, with a hint of sarcasm:

Polixenes: ... Is not your father grown incapable
Of reasonable affairs?[1] Is he not stupid
With age and altering rheums?[2] Can he speak? Hear?
Know man from man? Dispute his own estate?[3]
Lies he not bed-rid? And again does nothing
But what he did being childish?[4]

[1] *no longer able to behave rationally*
[2] *debilitating illnesses*
[3] *discuss his own condition*
[4] *has reverted to a second childhood*

Florizel replies that his father is in excellent health. Growing impatient, he maintains that there are good reasons why the planned marriage must not be revealed to his father. Polixenes continues to press him on the subject, and the shepherd too adds his voice.

The young man remains adamant, and orders the shepherd to witness their engagement. At this point the king reveals his true identity, and confronts his son furiously:

Florizel: … for some other reasons, my grave sir,
              Which 'tis not fit you know, I not acquaint
              My father of this business.
Polixenes: Let him know't.
Florizel: He shall not.
Polixenes: Prithee let him.
Florizel: No, he must not.
Shepherd: Let him, my son. He shall not need to grieve
              At knowing of thy choice.
Florizel: Come, come, he must not.
              Mark our contract.
Polixenes: [*removing his disguise*] Mark your divorce, young sir,
              Whom son I dare not call. Thou art too base
              To be acknowledged.

Florizel is not the only target of the king's anger. He believes that the shepherd was aware of the young man's true identity, and threatens to hang him for attempting to marry his daughter to a prince. As for Perdita herself, Polixenes warns her that he will destroy the beauty that has led his son astray:

Polixenes: [*to Shepherd*] Thou, old traitor,
              I am sorry that by hanging thee I can
              But shorten thy life one week.[1] [*to Perdita*] And thou,
                fresh piece
              Of excellent witchcraft,[2] whom of force[3] must know
              The royal fool thou cop'st with[4] –
Shepherd: O, my heart!
Polixenes: I'll have thy beauty scratched with briars and made
              More homely than thy state.[5]

[1] *it's a shame that hanging you will do no more, at*
    your age, than shorten your life by a week
[2] *clever young enchantress*
[3] *inevitably, necessarily*
[4] *you are dealing with*
[5] *made more unattractive than your lowly status*

Polixenes orders his son to return to court, warning him that he will be disowned if he so much as mentions the shepherd girl ever again. Turning to the shepherd, he announces that his punishment, at least for the time being, is to be suspended: but his daughter, on pain of death, must never allow the prince into their cottage again.

With that, the king storms out, leaving the gathering in stunned silence.

Camillo proposes a solution

Perdita is the first to speak. The king's outburst didn't frighten her, she claims; in fact, she almost plucked up the courage to tell him that their cottage is no less worthy than his palace. However, she sees that the love between Florizel and herself must, as she had feared, come to an end:

> Perdita: Will't please you, sir, be gone?
> I told you what would come of this. Beseech you,
> Of your own state[1] take care. This dream of mine
> Being now awake, I'll queen it no inch farther,[2]
> But milk my ewes and weep.
>
> [1] *your well-being; also, your position as prince of Bohemia*
> [2] *I'll stop imagining I could become queen*

Camillo, who has remained behind, goes to the aid of Perdita's father, who is almost overcome with grief. The old shepherd, devastated by the king's threat to hang him, rebukes Florizel bitterly for his deception. He curses his daughter, too: she must have realised that exchanging vows of love with the king's son would end in disaster. He leaves, dejected and resigned to death.

Florizel is unmoved by Perdita's dismay. Nothing will deter him from his intention to marry her:

Florizel:	Why look you so upon me?
	I am but sorry, not afeard;[1] delayed,
	But nothing altered.[2] What I was, I am,
	More straining on for plucking back[3] ...

[1] *although I am saddened, I am not afraid*
[2] *not changed at all in my determination*
[3] *this setback has made me all the more eager to keep going*

Perdita has warned Florizel many times that their dream would end like this, she reminds him:

Perdita:	How often have I told you 'twould be thus?
	How often said my dignity[1] would last
	But till 'twere known?[2]

[1] *my status as the future wife of a prince*
[2] *only until the truth was known*

The prince assures Perdita, again, that his feelings will never change. He will fulfil his vow to marry her even if it means giving up his future as king of Bohemia. Camillo, abandoning his disguise, advises Florizel not to do anything rash. The young man, however, is resolved to follow his heart. He reveals that he has a ship ready and waiting at the nearby port, and has decided to set sail with his beloved. He does not intend to see his father again.

Camillo, thinking quickly, wonders whether he might turn the situation to his advantage. He still longs to return to Sicilia, his homeland, and to be reunited with his old master, king Leontes. He swiftly devises a plan that might achieve this goal; then, turning to the prince, he suggests that it may still be possible for him to marry Perdita and be reconciled with his father.

Florizel is keen to know more. Camillo first asks him where he intends to go once he is on board ship: the young man admits that he has no plan but to set sail and put himself at the mercy of fortune. Camillo suggests a destination:

Camillo: … make for Sicilia,
And there present yourself and your fair princess,
For so I see she must be, 'fore Leontes …
                              Methinks I see
Leontes opening his free[1] arms and weeping
His welcomes forth; asks thee there, 'Son, forgiveness!'
As 'twere i'th' father's person[2] …

[1] *generous, welcoming*
[2] *begs your forgiveness as if you were Polixenes himself*

Shakespeare's friend and rival playwright Ben Jonson believed that a play's language, characters and plot should all be based firmly in the real world. He is known to have been irritated by Shakespeare's addition of a coast to the landlocked Kingdom of Bohemia (equivalent to the present-day Czech Republic), complaining that it was more than a hundred miles from the nearest sea.

A notoriously opinionated and argumentative individual, Jonson seems to have been vexed by the popularity of *The Winter's Tale* and *The Tempest*, both of which included elements of fantasy and mysticism: in his *Bartholomew Fair* of 1614, he refers scathingly to 'Tales, Tempests and suchlike Drolleries'.

Most theatregoers, however, are not concerned about realism or geographical accuracy in a fable like *The Winter's Tale*. Some critics have even suggested that Shakespeare knowingly added the fictional coastline of Bohemia in order to provoke his more literal-minded rival.

Camillo's plan is that Florizel should visit Leontes as a representative of king Polixenes, sent on a mission to reconcile the two men. Although in truth the king will know nothing of the meeting, Camillo – as a close friend of both Polixenes and Leontes – will be able to advise Florizel on what he should say and do in order to make it seem that his visit has been authorised by the king.

The alternative would be for the couple to sail through uncharted seas and stay in unfamiliar countries, possibly facing suffering and poverty; their love might not be able to survive such an ordeal, warns Camillo. Perdita disagrees, claiming that hardship may wear down the body, but not the spirit. Camillo is impressed by the shepherd's daughter:

Perdita:	I think affliction may subdue the cheek,[1]
	But not take in the mind.[2]
Camillo:	Yea? Say you so?
	There shall not at your father's house these seven years
	Be born another such.[3]
Florizel:	My good Camillo,
	She's as forward of her breeding as
	She is i'th' rear our birth.[4]

[1] *make the cheek grow pale; weaken the body*
[2] *defeat the soul*
[3] *your father is unlikely ever to have another daughter like you*
[4] *she's far more noble than you would expect, given her upbringing and her humble background*

Florizel is uncertain about his visit to the king of Sicilia, and the impression he will make; if he leaves now, as planned, he has none of the trappings of royalty. Camillo reassures him that, as a native of Sicilia, he still possesses wealth and property in his homeland. He will ensure that Florizel and Perdita are presented to king Leontes in a manner fitting the future king and queen of Bohemia.

A change of clothes

Camillo briefly takes the couple aside. At this moment Autolycus passes by, gloating over his success at the sheep-shearing feast. He has sold all his song-sheets, trinkets and fake jewellery, and in the process was able to observe his customers closely:

> *Autolycus:* ... They throng[1] who should buy first, as if my trinkets had been hallowed and brought a benediction[2] to the buyer; by which means I saw whose purse was best in picture;[3] and what I saw, to my good use I remembered.
>
> [1] *jostle for, compete with one another*
> [2] *blessing*
> [3] *looked the most promising*

Later, while the guests turned their attention to the shepherd's son and his attempts at singing, Autolycus managed to steal several purses. He would have helped himself to every single one, he boasts, if the old shepherd had not come in, shaken by the king's angry words.

Camillo now returns with the young couple. Autolycus is terrified that his remarks have been overheard; to his relief, however, the nobleman approaches him amicably. He has a strange request for the pedlar:

> *Camillo:* How now, good fellow? Why shakest thou so? Fear not, man. Here's no harm intended to thee.
> *Autolycus:* I am a poor fellow, sir.
> *Camillo:* Why, be so still. Here's nobody will steal that from thee.[1] Yet, for the outside of thy poverty,[2] we must make an exchange. Therefore disease thee[3] instantly ...
>
> [1] *you can carry on being poor; no one will take that away from you*
> [2] *the outward expression of your poverty; your shabby garments*
> [3] *remove your clothes*

The pedlar and Florizel exchange clothes. Camillo also gives Autolycus some money, even though the prince's clothes are far better than his own. Perdita too must disguise herself by hiding her face under a broad hat. The two of them must get to their ship without being spotted, explains Camillo.

The two lovers hurry off in the direction of the harbour. Camillo then reveals exactly why he is sending them to visit king Leontes:

Camillo: What I do next shall be to tell the king
Of this escape, and whither they are bound;
Wherein my hope is I shall so prevail
To force him after, in whose company
I shall re-view Sicilia[1] ...

[1] *I hope I shall persuade him to follow them, so that I can accompany him and see Sicilia once again*

Autolycus, lingering in the background, is intrigued: clearly the prince is up to no good, and is making a hasty getaway. He ponders the possibility of informing the king. That would be the honourable thing to do, he concludes, so he decides against it:

Autolycus: If I thought it were a piece of honesty to acquaint the king withal,[1] I would not do't. I hold it the more knavery[2] to conceal it, and therein am I constant to my profession.[3]

[1] *with this information*
[2] *I consider it more deceitful*
[3] *true to my avowed occupation*

Another opportunity for Autolycus

Two more people now come on the scene. Autolycus steps aside, listening carefully. There are opportunities everywhere for the conscientious villain, he reflects:

> *Autolycus:* Here is more matter for a hot[1] brain. Every lane's end,[2] every shop, church, session,[3] hanging, yields a careful[4] man work.
>
> [1] *busy, creative*
> [2] *place where people gather to read public notices*
> [3] *court sitting*
> [4] *attentive*

The passers-by are the old shepherd and his simpleton son. They are carrying the items that the shepherd found sixteen years ago, when he first stumbled across the baby girl: a shawl of rich material, and a box containing letters from Antigonus, now dead, who abandoned the child on the orders of king Leontes.

The two men, still terrified by the furious threats uttered by king Polixenes at the sheep-shearing, have decided to tell the truth about Perdita. They reason that, since she is not the shepherd's true daughter, the shepherd cannot be punished for her offence of leading the prince astray:

> *Clown:* She being none of your flesh and blood, your flesh and blood has not offended the king, and so your flesh and blood is not to be punished by him. Show those things you found about[1] her, those secret things ... This being done, let the law go whistle, I warrant you.[2]
>
> [1] *around, next to*
> [2] *the law can't touch you, I guarantee*

Autolycus is unsure of what to do. After a moment's thought, however, he concludes that his main aim must be to please prince Florizel; he was once a servant in the prince's house, and with luck might eventually get his old job back.

The best thing to do, he decides, is to keep these two away from the king. He steps out in front of them, assuming the role of an officious courtier. The fact that he is wearing Florizel's clothes gives him an air of sophistication, and they fail to recognise him as the pedlar who was at their sheep-shearing feast:

Autolycus: How now, rustics, whither are you bound?
Shepherd: To th' palace, an it like[1] your worship.
Autolycus: Your affairs there? What? With whom? The condition
of that fardel?[2] The place of your dwelling? Your
names? Your ages? Of what having, breeding, and
anything that is fitting to be known, discover![3]
Clown: We are but plain fellows, sir.

[1] *if it please*
[2] *the nature of that bundle you're carrying*
[3] *give details of your wealth, your background, and anything else that it is necessary for me to know*

"In the first half of the play, nature and natural passions prevail in that most artful of milieux, the court. In the second half, art prevails in the natural world of pastoral shepherds. It is art of a rather special kind, and its touchstone is Autolycus ... Three times he acts a part by disguising himself as what he is not, and each time his disguise succeeds in using art to conceal nature – and to precisely the same audience each time."

Andrew Gurr, *The Bear, the Statue, and Hysteria in* The Winter's Tale, 1983

Autolycus assures them that, if they wish to deal with the king, they need the help of a high-ranking nobleman such as himself. Learning that they are heading for the palace, he decides to divert them, sending them instead in the direction of the king's son Florizel:

> *Autolycus:* The king is not at the palace; he is gone aboard a new ship to purge melancholy and air himself;[1] for, if thou beest capable of things serious,[2] thou must know the king is full of grief.
>
> [1] *to take the sea air and rid himself of his sorrow*
> [2] *if you are able to comprehend important matters*

The shepherd is only too aware that it is Florizel's infatuation with Perdita that has upset the king. Autolycus confirms that Perdita's father, wherever he may be, is in serious trouble:

> *Autolycus:* If that shepherd be not in handfast, let him fly;[1] the curses he shall have, the tortures he shall feel, will break the back of man, the heart of monster.
>
> [1] *if has not yet been arrested, he'd better run away at once*

Without giving away his identity, the shepherd's son asks nervously about his own fate. Autolycus assures him that he king's displeasure extends to the whole family:

> *Clown:* Has the old man e'er a son, sir, do you hear, an't like you,[1] sir?
> *Autolycus:* He has a son, who shall be flayed[2] alive, then 'nointed over with honey, set on the head of a wasps' nest, then stand till he be three-quarters-and-a-dram[3] dead ...
>
> [1] *have you heard any suggestion that the old shepherd has a son, if you don't mind my asking*
> [2] *have his skin stripped off*
> [3] *almost completely*

The two men listen with horror to the catalogue of torments that awaits them. Autolycus, still pretending not to know who they are, comments cheerfully that the infamous shepherd and his son deserve to be punished for trying to demean the royal family of Bohemia.

Changing the subject, he offers to help the two strangers. Hinting that a suitable reward is expected, he proposes to take them to the king's ship, bring them into the royal presence and speak on their behalf. The offer is hastily accepted:

Autolycus: Tell me – for you seem to be honest plain men – what you have to the king.[1] Being something gently considered,[2] I'll bring you where he is aboard, tender your persons to his presence, whisper him in your behalfs, and if it be in man, besides the king, to effect your suits,[3] here is man shall do it.

Clown: [*aside to Shepherd*] He seems to be of great authority. Close[4] with him, give him gold …

[1] *what your business is, why you want to see the king*
[2] *if I am rewarded in keeping with my noble status*
[3] *if anyone other than the king himself can grant your request*
[4] *come to terms, make a deal*

The shepherd hands over some gold, promising that there will be more when they have spoken to the king. He and his son are both hugely relieved that they will be able to put their case to Polixenes, and the young man pledges even more gold:

Clown: [*aside to Shepherd*] He must know 'tis none of your daughter,[1] nor my sister. We are gone else.[2]
[*to Autolycus*] Sir, I will give you as much as this old man does when the business is performed …

[1] *the king must be told that Perdita is definitely not your daughter*
[2] *we are finished otherwise*

The three of them set off for the harbour. Autolycus is in high spirits. Florizel will surely be grateful to hear the shepherd's revelations, he reasons, in which case the prince may offer to employ him as his servant once again. In any case, he will have plenty of gold to show for his hard work.

Haunted by the past

V, i

Back in Sicilia, king Leontes is still brooding on the terrible events of the past, brought about by his own folly: the loss of his son, the rejection of his baby daughter, his estrangement from his old friend Polixenes and, above all, the death of his wife Hermione.

His courtiers try to persuade him to bring his grieving to an end, for his own good and that of the kingdom:

> *Cleomenes:* Sir, you have done enough, and have performed
> A saint-like sorrow. No fault could you make
> Which you have not redeemed;[1] indeed, paid down
> More penitence than done trespass.[2] At the last[3]
> Do as the heavens have done, forget your evil;
> With them, forgive yourself.
>
> [1] *there is no sin you could commit that you have not already atoned for*
> [2] *you have punished yourself even more than your offences warranted*
> [3] *finally*

One voice, however, cannot refrain from reminding the king of the wife he has lost. It is that of Paulina, whose husband Antigonus is also presumed to have died. She cannot forget the queen's exceptional qualities, nor Leontes' cruelty in causing her death:

> *Paulina:* If one by one you wedded all the world,
> Or from the all that are[1] took something good
> To make a perfect woman, she you killed
> Would be unparalleled.[2]
>
> [1] *from every woman now alive*
> [2] *would still be without equal*

The courtiers reproach Paulina for failing to comfort the king. They remind her that the kingdom is without an heir; the king's son Mamillius is dead, and his daughter too must have perished when she was abandoned in the wilderness many years ago. It is time for Leontes to marry again, they believe.

Paulina retorts that no woman is worthy enough to replace Hermione. She reminds the others of the words of the oracle:

> Paulina: … has not the divine Apollo said?
> Is't not the tenor[1] of his oracle
> That king Leontes shall not have an heir
> Till his lost child be found? Which that it shall
> Is all as monstrous[2] to our human reason
> As my Antigonus to break his grave
> And come again to me; who, on my life,
> Did perish with the infant.

> [1] *content, message*
> [2] *the idea that the abandoned child will be found is as inconceivable*

It would be blasphemous, she suggests, for the king to ignore the will of the heavens and have another child. Leontes finds her argument persuasive and, despite complaints from his advisers, resolves that he will never marry again.

Eventually Paulina relents slightly, and they come to a compromise: the king may one day choose another wife, but only with Paulina's blessing.

Unexpected news

The discussion is interrupted when a gentleman suddenly enters, bringing an urgent and surprising message: prince Florizel, son of king Polixenes, has arrived at the palace, along with his princess. Leontes is taken aback:

Leontes: ... He comes not
            Like to his father's greatness.[1] His approach,
            So out of circumstance[2] and sudden, tells us
            'Tis not a visitation framed,[3] but forced
            By need and accident. What train?[4]
Gentleman: But few,
            And those but mean.[5]
Leontes: His princess, say you, with him?
Gentleman: Ay, the most peerless piece of earth,[6] I think,
            That e'er the sun shone bright on.

> [1] in a manner appropriate to the son of a king
> [2] lacking in formality
> [3] a planned visit
> [4] what entourage is accompanying him?
> [5] just a few people of low rank
> [6] incomparable human being

Paulina rebukes the gentleman, remarking that he would once have praised Hermione in the same terms. He apologises, but assures her that she too will be impressed by the princess. Turning to Leontes, Paulina points out that his son, had he lived, would be the same age as the young prince who is about to visit them. Leontes begs her not to mention the subject; remembering the boy's death still causes him unbearable distress.

Florizel and Perdita are now ushered into the king's presence. When Leontes sees the prince, he is overcome with nostalgia, recalling how close he and the young Polixenes used to be:

Leontes: Were I but twenty-one,
            Your father's image is so hit[1] in you,
            His very air, that I should call you brother,
            As I did him ...

> [1] copied so exactly

It was through his own recklessness that their friendship ended, admits Leontes, but he would give anything for the two of them to be reunited. Florizel brings hopeful news:

Leontes: … I lost –
All mine own folly – the society,
Amity too, of your brave father,[1] whom,
Though bearing misery, I desire my life
Once more to look on him.[2]
Florizel: By his command
Have I here touched[3] Sicilia …

[1] *the company and friendship of your noble father*
[2] *although I'm burdened with grief, I want to live to see him once more*
[3] *made landfall on*

The prince tells Leontes that Polixenes had wanted to come to Sicilia in person to renew their friendship; however, the infirmities of age prevented him from undertaking the voyage himself. Instead, he has sent his son to bring his message of love and reconciliation.

In the eighteenth century, *Florizel and Perdita*, a romanticised, pastoral version of *The Winter's Tale* from which all the tragic elements had been removed, was very popular. In 1779, King George III took his 17-year-old son, the Prince of Wales, to see a performance. The young man immediately fell passionately in love with Mary Robinson, the actress playing Perdita.

Over the following months, the prince sent a succession of ardent love-letters, signing himself 'Florizel', and a love affair eventually ensued. The 22-year old Mary soon became a celebrity, and her extravagant lifestyle attracted fascination and disapproval in equal measure.

The affair lasted less than a year, and Mary was left with crippling debts. The prince provided some financial support – mainly due to Mary's threat to publish his love-letters – and Mary went on to make a living as a successful poet and novelist. However, her finances were always precarious, and she died in poverty at the age of 44.

Even more unexpected news

Leontes is joyful to hear from his friend, but painfully aware of his own responsibility for the rift between them, and his failure to address it. He cries out to the absent Polixenes before turning to his son:

Leontes: Good gentleman, the wrongs I have done thee stir
Afresh within me, and these thy offices,
So rarely kind, are as interpreters
Of my behindhand slackness.[1] [*to Florizel*] Welcome hither,
As is the spring to th'earth!

> [1] *your greetings, so wonderfully kind, serve as a comment on my negligence*

Leontes is surprised that the young princess has been exposed to the dangers of the sea-crossing from Bohemia. Florizel – perhaps following a story agreed earlier with Camillo – explains that they have in fact crossed, on gentle southerly winds, from north Africa: his wife is the daughter of a Libyan warlord. This is why they have so few attendants, he reveals: most of the courtiers in their retinue have returned to Bohemia, to tell the king of the couple's safe arrival from Libya.

Welcoming the prince and his wife, Leontes cannot help remembering his own lost children. The two young people now in front of him force him to contemplate his unhappy situation:

Leontes: You have a holy father,
A graceful gentleman, against whose person,
So sacred as it is, I have done sin,
For which the heavens, taking angry note,
Have left me issueless[1] ...
                    What might I have been,
Might I a son and daughter now have looked on,
Such goodly things as you?

> [1] *childless, without an heir*

The mood suddenly changes when another unexpected message arrives, even more startling than the last:

> Lord: Please you, great sir,
> Bohemia greets you from himself,[1] by me;
> Desires you to attach[2] his son, who has,
> His dignity and duty both cast off,[3]
> Fled from his father, from his hopes, and with
> A shepherd's daughter.

[1] *king Polixenes greets you personally*
[2] *arrest*
[3] *having abandoned both the decorum appropriate to a prince and his duty as a son*

In short, Polixenes is far from being confined to his bed in Bohemia as Florizel claimed. At this very moment the king is in Sicilia, in hot pursuit of his delinquent son; and that son has not married a Libyan noblewoman, but has eloped with a common shepherd girl.

Fifty years after Shakespeare's death, tastes had changed considerably. The fashion was for witty, elegant comedies on contemporary themes; and although Shakespeare was still admired, his work could seem bizarre, primitive and unrefined to modern sensibilities. The verdict of a major playwright of the time – later to become the first Poet Laureate – summed up the general opinion:

"Poetry was then, if not in its infancy, at least not arrived to its present vigour and maturity ... many of Shakespeare's plays, such as The Winter's Tale, *were either grounded on impossibilities, or at least so meanly written, that the comedy neither caused your mirth, nor the serious part your concernment."*

John Dryden, *Defense of the Epilogue*, 1672

A plea for help

The messenger reports another curious detail: the king and his adviser Camillo, hastening towards Leontes' palace, came across the father and the brother of the supposed princess, who had been on the same ship as Florizel. The two countrymen have desperately been trying to explain something to Polixenes, but he refuses to listen, threatening them with terrible punishments.

Florizel is horrified: his trusted friend Camillo has betrayed him, and informed the king of his escape to Sicilia. Perdita too is deeply distressed, both by her father's predicament and by the fact that their marriage plans have again been thwarted.

Leontes, finding they are not married as the prince had claimed, enquires further about his partner. It is a shame, he feels, that Perdita's lowly background means that they cannot marry:

> *Leontes:*   My lord,
> Is this the daughter of a king?
> *Florizel:*   She is,
> When once she is my wife.
> *Leontes:*   That 'once', I see, by your good father's speed
> Will come on very slowly.[1] I am sorry,
> Most sorry, you have broken from his liking,
> Where you were tied in duty,[2] and as sorry
> Your choice is not so rich in worth as beauty,
> That you might well enjoy her.[3]

> [1] *your father's imminent arrival means that your marriage may never take place*
> [2] *you have incurred the displeasure of the man you were duty-bound to obey*
> [3] *your beloved's status, which is far inferior to her beauty, means that you cannot have her as your wife*

Florizel reassures Perdita that nothing will alter his love for her. He turns to Leontes, and asks him to remember his own experience of love as a young man. As an old friend, he is ideally placed to influence Polixenes, and perhaps to persuade him to agree to his son's longed-for marriage.

Leontes finds himself distracted by the young shepherd girl who has been treated so dismissively by king Polixenes. Paulina admonishes him, and he apologises, claiming that the girl unaccountably brings to mind his wife Hermione:

Florizel: … at your request,
My father will grant precious things as trifles.
Leontes: Would he do so, I'd beg your precious mistress,
Which he counts but a trifle.[1]
Paulina: Sir, my liege,
Your eye hath too much youth in't. Not a month
'Fore your queen died, she was more worth such gazes
Than what you look on now.
Leontes: I thought of her
Even in these looks I made.[2]

[1] *if that were the case, I'd ask for your sweetheart,*
   whom Polixenes has rejected
[2] *I was thinking of Hermione when I looked at this*
   young lady

Returning to the subject of Florizel's request, Leontes agrees to help. He sympathises with the young couple, and promises that he will do his best to persuade Polixenes to give his blessing to their marriage.

An emotional reunion V, ii

Leontes' palace is a hive of activity. The king, his courtiers, Paulina, and the newly arrived Florizel and Perdita are all present: and they have been joined by king Polixenes, in pursuit of his wayward son, accompanied by his trusted adviser Camillo. The old shepherd and his son, carrying their valuable bundle, have also gained entry.

Outside the palace, Autolycus is waiting, trying to glean whatever scraps of information he can. A gentleman coming out of the palace reports that the old shepherd has revealed some important news, but is unsure of the contents.

Two more gentlemen now arrive in quick succession. The first has heard that Florizel's companion is indeed king Leontes' long-lost daughter. The next was present at the dramatic moment when the shepherd opened his bundle to reveal the items he found, all those years ago, alongside the baby girl:

> *2nd Gentleman:* ... The oracle is fulfilled, the king's daughter is found ... This news which is called true is so like an old tale that the verity of it is in strong suspicion.[1] Has the king found his heir?
>
> *3rd Gentleman:* Most true ... The mantle[2] of queen Hermione's; her jewel about the neck of it; the letters of Antigonus found with it, which they know to be his character;[3] the majesty of the creature,[4] in resemblance of the mother ... and many other evidences proclaim her with all certainty to be the king's daughter.
>
> [1] *it's hard to believe that it really is true*
> [2] *shawl, cloak (in which the baby girl was wrapped)*
> [3] *handwriting*
> [4] *young woman*

The scene was one of intense emotion, report the gentlemen, with Leontes' joy at finding his daughter alive, his grief at the memory of his wife's death, and both kings' euphoria at the renewal of their friendship. Camillo, too, was overwhelmed to find himself back in his homeland, at last, with his old master; even the old shepherd was crying tears of happiness.

The shepherd's son, it emerges, had kept a handkerchief and a ring when he buried the remains of Antigonus, killed by the bear in the Bohemian wilderness. These confirmed Paulina's fears about her husband's fate, but she was comforted by the fact that the baby girl had been rescued from her hostile surroundings. The gentleman describes how she clasped Perdita warmly in her arms:

> *3rd Gentleman:* ... O, the noble combat that 'twixt joy and
> sorrow was fought in Paulina! She had one eye
> declined for the loss of her husband, another elevated
> that the oracle was fulfilled. She lifted the princess
> from the earth, and so locks her in embracing as if she
> would pin her to her heart, that she might no more be
> in danger of losing.[1]
>
> [1] *so that Perdita would never again be in danger of*
> *becoming lost*

The most moving event of all came when Leontes, wracked with sorrow and guilt, told Perdita of the death of her mother Hermione. Her anguish was shared by everyone present:

> *3rd Gentleman:* ... from one sign of dolour[1] to another she did,
> with an 'Alas', I would fain say[2] bleed tears; for I am
> sure my heart wept blood. Who was most marble there
> changed colour.[3] Some swooned, all sorrowed. If all
> the world could have seen't, the woe had been[4]
> universal.
>
> [1] *expression of grief*
> [2] *I can only describe it as*
> [3] *even the most hard-hearted onlookers were affected*
> [4] *would have been*

One of the gentlemen mentions that the entire company has now left the king's audience chamber. Paulina has commissioned a famous sculptor, renowned for his ability to fashion perfect likenesses, to create a statue of queen Hermione: and all the guests, eager to see this lifelike monument, are now on their way to view it.

Another gentleman remarks that Paulina has been a regular visitor to the secluded house in which the statue stands, although he had not previously known the reason:

> *2nd Gentleman:* I thought she had some great matter there in hand, for she hath privately twice or thrice a day, ever since the death of Hermione, visited that removed[1] house.
>
> [1] *remote, isolated*

All three gentlemen decide to set off for Paulina's house without further delay.

In Shakespeare's time, play scripts were the property of the theatre company for which they were written. They were a valuable asset, and companies were generally unwilling to publish them, particularly while a play was still popular and attracting audiences. At least half of Shakespeare's plays, for example, were not published during his lifetime.

In time, however, plays gradually came to be regarded, like poetry, as valid works of literature. Five years after Shakespeare's death, John Heminges and Henry Condell, two of his fellow-actors, set about the task of creating a complete edition of Shakespeare's plays, including introductory material and an engraving of the author. The resulting book, now known as the 'First Folio', was published in 1623. This collected edition contained many plays – including *Macbeth*, *Julius Caesar*, *The Tempest* and *The Winter's Tale* – which would otherwise have been lost for ever.

Going up in the world

Autolycus, now alone, reflects that he has not been able to profit from recent events. Although he was the one who arranged for the old shepherd and his son to be on board Florizel's ship, his attempts to speak to the prince about the shepherds and their discovery came to nothing; the young man was preoccupied with his sweetheart, who was suffering from terrible seasickness.

He is philosophical, however, about his lack of success. Even if he had managed to discover the truth about Perdita's birth, and reveal it to the young couple, his reputation is so bad that he would have received little credit. Instead, the shepherds themselves have been rewarded handsomely for their discovery and nurturing of the king's daughter; Leontes has given them the official title of gentlemen.

At this point the two of them approach, wearing the finery appropriate to their new status:

> *Autolycus:* Here come those I have done good to against my will, and already appearing in the blossoms of their fortune.[1]
>
> [1] *the first flowering of their prosperity; their refined clothes*

The shepherd is explaining to his son that any children he has will not only be gentlemen, but 'gentlemen born'. The simple-minded young man, taken with the phrase, decides it applies to him too. Seeing Autolycus, he challenges the pedlar to accuse him now of lying, as he has done in the past; as a gentleman born, he will be bound to defend his honour.

The response pleases the young man, and he goes on to describe, in his confused way, the scene when Perdita's true identity was revealed:

> *Clown:* Give me the lie,[1] do, and try[2] whether I am not now a gentleman born.
>
> *Autolycus:* I know you are now, sir, a gentleman born.
>
> *Clown:* Ay, and have been so any time these four hours.
>
> *Shepherd:* And so have I, boy.
>
> *Clown:* So you have; but I was a gentleman born before my father, for the king's son took me by the hand and called me brother, and then the two kings called my father brother, and then the prince my brother and the princess my sister called my father father, and so we wept; and there was the first gentleman-like tears that ever we shed.
>
> *Shepherd:* We may live, son, to shed many more.
>
> *Clown:* Ay, or else 'twere hard luck[3] ...

> [1] *accuse me of lying*
> [2] *test, find out*
> [3] *I hope we will; it would be a shame if we didn't*

Autolycus, still hoping to be employed once more in prince Florizel's household, asks the two gentlemen to put in a good word for him. They graciously agree, as long as he promises to mend his ways. Then, hearing the various courtiers and members of the royal families making their way to see the statue of Hermione, the shepherds set off for Paulina's house. They invite Autolycus to join them:

> *Clown:* Hark, the kings and the princes, our kindred,[1] are going to see the queen's picture. Come, follow us. We'll be thy good masters.

> [1] *relations, family*

A spellbinding sight

Paulina's house is thronged with guests, all eager to see the statue of the queen. When the king thanks her for her help over the years, she admits that she has not always been tactful:

Leontes: O grave and good Paulina, the great comfort
That I have had of thee!
Paulina: What, sovereign sir,
I did not well,[1] I meant well.

[1] *even when I failed to act properly*

Paulina thanks the king for favouring her house not only with his own presence, but also with that of king Polixenes, his son the prince, and the future princess. Leontes reminds her, gently, that they have come to see the statue of his dead wife Hermione. Paulina explains that she keeps it hidden from public view, behind a curtain:

Paulina: As she lived peerless,[1]
So her dead likeness[2] I do well believe
Excels whatever yet you looked upon,
Or hand of man hath done. Therefore I keep it
Lonely, apart.

[1] *in life she had no equal*
[2] *her lifeless image*

In a dramatic gesture, Paulina now walks over to the curtain and pulls it back. The guests look on, stunned, as the astoundingly lifelike image of the queen is revealed.

The king eventually breaks the silence. He wishes the statue could rebuke him, as he deserves, so that he might hear Hermione's voice again. Then it occurs to him that this was not in her nature:

> Paulina: Comes it not something near?[1]
> Leontes: Her natural posture.
> Chide me, dear stone, that[2] I may say indeed
> Thou art Hermione – or, rather, thou art she
> In thy not chiding;[3] for she was as tender
> As infancy and grace.[4]

[1] *rather close to the real Hermione*
[2] *so that*
[3] *the fact that you are not reprimanding me makes you even more realistic*
[4] *as gentle as a child, and as divine mercy*

Leontes notices that the statue seems older than the Hermione he remembers; this is part of the sculptor's artistry, replies Paulina. Remembering his love for Hermione, Leontes feels her loss more keenly than ever.

Chide me, dear stone ...

"The hardened image of his wife forces him to turn his gaze inward upon his own hard heart. The play ends with the melting of that heart and the rekindling of love ..."

Jonathan Bate, *Soul of the Age*, 2009

Perdita, too, is transfixed by the image of her mother, of whom she has no memory. She moves to touch the statue, but Paulina hastily warns her away:

Perdita: … give me leave,[1]
And do not say 'tis superstition, that
I kneel and then implore her blessing. Lady,
Dear queen, that ended when I but began,[2]
Give me that hand of yours to kiss.
Paulina: O patience!
The statue is but newly fixed;[3] the colour's
Not dry.

[1] *allow me*
[2] *whose life ended when mine had just begun*
[3] *finished, painted*

Camillo and Polixenes, seeing Leontes' distress, try to comfort him. He has suffered enough, they believe, and must not allow his life to be blighted any longer by grief and remorse. Paulina offers to draw the curtain shut again, but Leontes brushes the thought aside, and continues to study the statue intently:

Leontes: Do not draw the curtain.
Paulina: No longer shall you gaze on't, lest your fancy
May think anon it moves.[1]
Leontes: Let be,[2] let be!
                                    … See, my lord,
Would you not deem[3] it breathed, and that those veins
Did verily bear blood?
Polixenes: Masterly done.
The very life seems warm upon her lip.
Leontes: The fixture of her eye has motion in't,
As we are mocked with art.[4]

[1] *in case your imagination should soon tell you that
    it's moving*
[2] *leave the curtain alone*
[3] *judge*
[4] *her eye, though only painted, seems to move, as if
    the sculptor's artistry were playing with our senses*

Paulina again offers to pull the curtain shut and remove the statue from view, but Leontes is resolute. The image of his lost love torments him, but he is irresistibly drawn to it:

> *Leontes:*   … this affliction has a taste as sweet
> As any cordial comfort.[1] Still methinks
> There is an air comes from her. What fine chisel
> Could ever yet cut breath? Let no man mock me,
> For I will kiss her.

> [1] *soothing medicine*

Paulina hurriedly prevents the king from approaching the statue, and yet again suggests that the curtain should be drawn to prevent further distress. Leontes again insists on keeping the statue in sight, however, and Perdita too cannot take her eyes off it.

Back to life

Paulina now makes a startling announcement: she will make the statue move, and come down from its pedestal. She denies that she is using evil powers, and asks anyone who distrusts her to leave.

Leontes declares, with certainty, that everyone will stay to witness the event. Paulina addresses the statue:

> *Paulina:*   It is required
> You do awake your faith. Then all stand still.
> Or those that think it is unlawful business
> I am about, let them depart.
> *Leontes:*   Proceed.
> No foot shall stir.
> *Paulina:*   Music, awake her; strike! [*music plays*]
> 'Tis time; descend; be stone no more; approach.
> … Bequeath to death your numbness, for from him
> Dear life redeems you.[1]

> [1] *abandon your state of immobility and leave it to*
> *death; precious life is rescuing you*

> "Leontes, at first, wanted to possess a Hermione who was, in effect, a statue. He had distrusted her wit, her warmth, her blood ... Now he explicitly longs for her warm life, her blood, her breath, her speech. His determination to kiss the statue signals to Paulina that he is ready for reunion with the woman Hermione. The moment of reunion is as painful, laborious, and exhilarating as the moment of birth."
>
> Carol Thomas Neely, *Broken Nuptials*, 1993

The statue moves; and Hermione, now alive, approaches her husband. At first he is wary but, encouraged by Paulina, he clasps her hand, and they embrace silently and tenderly:

Paulina: Nay, present your hand.
            When she was young, you wooed her; now in age,
            Is she become the suitor? [1]
Leontes: O, she's warm!
            If this be magic, let it be an art
            Lawful as eating.
Polixenes: She embraces him.
Camillo: She hangs about his neck …

            [1] *is she now obliged to pursue you?*

Hermione is clearly alive, but has not yet spoken. She will speak, says Paulina, when her daughter comes forward. Perdita now kneels in front of her mother, and Hermione cries out to the gods in joy and gratitude. She has many questions for her child, whom she last saw as a new-born baby:

Paulina: Turn, good lady,
            Our Perdita is found.
Hermione: You gods, look down,
            And from your sacred vials[1] pour your graces
            Upon my daughter's head! Tell me, mine own,
            Where hast thou been preserv'd?[2] Where liv'd? How found
            Thy father's court?

            [1] *vessels*
            [2] *kept safe*

Answers to all these questions, and more, will come later, says Paulina. For now, they should all share the joy of the present. Although events have produced a happy resolution for many of them, she adds, her own future holds nothing but mourning for her lost husband Antigonus:

> *Paulina:*   I, an old turtle,[1]
> Will wing me to some withered bough, and there
> My mate, that's never to be found again,
> Lament till I am lost.
>
> [1] *turtle dove*

Leontes interrupts Paulina's sad musings with a surprising proposal. He reminds her that not long ago, when he believed Hermione to be dead, he agreed that he would only marry again with Paulina's approval. The tables are now turned: Paulina has, miraculously, found Leontes' wife, and it is now his turn to find her a husband. He knows just the man, and has already made some discreet enquiries:

> *Leontes:*   Thou hast found mine,[1]
> But how is to be questioned, for I saw her,
> As I thought, dead, and have in vain said many
> A prayer upon her grave. I'll not seek far –
> For him, I partly know his mind[2] – to find thee
> An honourable husband. Come, Camillo,
> And take her by the hand …
>
> [1] *my wife Hermione*
> [2] *as for the man in question, I'm reasonably well aware of his feelings*

Camillo and Paulina join hands.

> "The Winter's Tale ... *is a profound lyrical meditation on the theme of forgiveness and renewal, full of delicacy and beauty, yet always close to the earth and the human heartbeat. Shakespeare never wrote a more perfect work.*"
>
> John Wain, *The Living World of Shakespeare*, 1964

Turning back to Hermione, Leontes encourages her to renew her affection for Polixenes. He regrets ever having mistrusted them:

Leontes: ... Look upon my brother.[1] Both your pardons,
That e'er I put between your holy looks
My ill suspicion.

[1] *my close friend; Polixenes*

Finally, the king introduces Hermione to Polixenes' son Florizel, soon to marry Perdita and become their son-in-law. A great deal has happened since the terrible rift of sixteen years ago, reflects Leontes. They all have many questions to ask, and many stories to tell:

Leontes: Good Paulina,
Lead us from hence, where we may leisurely
Each one demand and answer to his part
Performed[1] in this wide gap of time since first
We were dissevered.[2] Hastily lead away.

[1] *we may all, in our own time, discuss the part we have played*
[2] *cut off from one another, separated*

The time has come to leave the sorrows of the past behind. Paulina leads the way, and the gathering departs in high spirits.

Acknowledgements

The following publications have proved invaluable as sources of factual information and critical insight:

- Catharine Arnold, *Globe: Life in Shakespeare's London*, Simon & Schuster, 2015

- Jonathan Bate, *Soul of the Age*, Penguin, 2009

- Charles Boyce, *Shakespeare A to Z*, Roundtable Press, 1990

- Terry Eagleton, *William Shakespeare*, Blackwell, 1986

- Gareth Lloyd Evans, *Shakespeare 1606 – 1616*, Oliver and Boyd, 1973

- Nicholas Fogg, *Hidden Shakespeare*, Amberley Publishing, 2013

- Levi Fox, *The Shakespeare Handbook*, Bodley Head, 1987

- Charles Frey, *Shakespeare's Vast Romance*, University of Missouri Press, 1980

- Northrop Frye, *On Shakespeare*, Yale University Press, 1986

- Andrew Gurr, *The Bear, the Statue, and Hysteria in* The Winter's Tale, in *Shakespeare Quarterly*, Johns Hopkins University Press, 1983

- Coppélia Kahn, *Representing Shakespeare: New Psychoanalytic Essays*, Johns Hopkins University Press, 1980

- Laurie Maguire and Emma Smith, *30 Great Myths About Shakespeare*, Wiley-Blackwell, 2013

- John Masefield, *William Shakespeare*, Oxford University Press, 1911

- Carol Thomas Neely, *Broken Nuptials in Shakespeare's Plays*, Yale University Press, 1993

- John Pitcher, Introduction to the Arden Shakespeare edition of *The Winter's Tale*, Bloomsbury Publishing, 2010

- John Wain, *The Living World of Shakespeare*, Penguin, 1964

- Michael Wood, *In Search of Shakespeare*, BBC Books, 2005

- David Young, *The Heart's Forest*, Yale University Press, 1972

All quotations from *The Winter's Tale* are taken from the Arden Shakespeare.

Guides currently available in the *Shakespeare Handbooks* series are:

- ❏ **Antony & Cleopatra** (ISBN 978 1 899747 02 3)
- ❏ **As You Like It** (ISBN 978 1 899747 00 9)
- ❏ **The Comedy of Errors** (ISBN 978 1 899747 16 0)
- ❏ **Cymbeline** (ISBN 978 1 899747 20 7)
- ❏ **Hamlet** (ISBN 978 1 899747 07 8)
- ❏ **Henry IV, Part 1** (ISBN 978 1 899747 05 4)
- ❏ **Julius Caesar** (ISBN 978 1 899747 11 5)
- ❏ **King Lear** (ISBN 978 1 899747 03 0)
- ❏ **Macbeth** (ISBN 978 1 899747 04 7)
- ❏ **Measure for Measure** (ISBN 978 1 899747 14 6)
- ❏ **The Merchant of Venice** (ISBN 978 1 899747 13 9)
- ❏ **The Merry Wives of Windsor** (ISBN 978 1 899747 18 4)
- ❏ **A Midsummer Night's Dream** (ISBN 978 1 899747 09 2)
- ❏ **Much Ado About Nothing** (ISBN 978 1 899747 17 7)
- ❏ **Othello** (ISBN 978 1 899747 12 2)
- ❏ **Richard II** (ISBN 978 1 899747 19 1)
- ❏ **Romeo & Juliet** (ISBN 978 1 899747 10 8)
- ❏ **The Tempest** (ISBN 978 1 899747 08 5)
- ❏ **Twelfth Night** (ISBN 978 1 899747 01 6)
- ❏ **The Winter's Tale** (ISBN 978 1 899747 15 3)

www.shakespeare-handbooks.com